It's Time to Be Bold

Michael W. Smith

WORD PUBLISHING
Nashville·London·Vancouver·Melbourne

It's Time to Be Bold

Unless otherwise noted, Scripture quotations used in this book are
from The Holy Bible: New International Version. Copyright © 1973,
1978, 1984, International Bible Society. Used by permission of
Zondervan Bible Publishers.

Other Scripture references are from the following sources:
The Living Bible (TLB), copyright © 1971
by Tyndale House Publishers, Wheaton, IL.
Used by permission.

The New King James Version (NKJV),
copyright © 1979, 1980, 1982, 1992,
Thomas Nelson, Inc., Publisher.

The King James Version of the Bible (KJV).

Library of Congress Cataloging-in-Publication Data

Smith, Michael W. (Michael Whitaker)
It's time to be bold / Michael W. Smith
p.   cm.
ISBN 0-8499-3336-6 (trade paper)
1. Christian life.   2. Smith, Michael W. (Michael Whitaker)
I. Title.
BV4501.2.S53495   1997
248.4–dc21
97-26522
CIP

Printed in the United States of America
7 8 9 0 1 2 3 4 5 QBP 9 8 7 6 5 4 3 2 1

Contents

Acknowledgments

In music the lead singer gets all of the attention
. . . in football it's the quarterback. But, it's the
support people that truly make it all work. I want
to thank the "team" that made this book possible.

Bob Laurent—You are a good and faithful
friend. Pulling this book together had to be
more work than you anticipated. I hope that
its effect on kids will prove to have been worth
your time.

Sean Hedegard—You added a consistency
and a continuity to this book that only you
could have provided. You know me well and I
appreciate your friendship.

Mike Nolan—Sometimes I think you have
read my diary. You have the amazing ability to
help me clearly communicate what is on the
inside. You are a gifted writer and make the
process painless.

Introduction

It's Time to Be Bold

"When I called, you answered me;
you made me bold and bravehearted."
— King David

You could feel the threat of violence, like sharks gathering for a feeding frenzy. It was a reckless kind of spiritual darkness that was almost tangible. Things were getting out of control, and my view from the center of the stage told me there wasn't a single policeman around.

A heavy roll of duct tape flew up from the crowd and ricocheted off my chest. Still, I kept singing,

> *On the wire*
> *Balancing your dreams*
> *Hoping ends will meet their means . . .*[1]

This is crazy! my mind screamed. *What am I doing here?*

> *You feel alone*
> *Uninspired . . .*

Honestly, I felt like I had been thrown to the lions. *These people don't want to hear me*

1

tonight. Another large object whistled past my head, hurled by someone who didn't appreciate my choice of songs. *What is going on?* I wondered, stopping momentarily. *I should be at home putting my kids to bed right now, or anywhere but here.*

But even as my panic and frustration built, my pride shouted them down. *They're not going to beat me,* I told myself. *Nobody's making me quit. Not now. Not ever. I'm going to finish this song!*

In retrospect, I should have read the situation better. I'd already had the feeling that this was not going to be a typical concert. Instead of being drawn by my songs, they were simply coming to party. Because the legal drinking age in the state was only eighteen, the event was seen as just another excuse to get wild with hundreds of other high school students.

The way I figured it, most of them had been drinking and partying for more than three hours before I took the stage. I had made a split-second decision to sing something with a message, a song that would encourage them, instead of trying to compete with the hard-core bands that were on before me. Now it looked like I was paying for that decision.

Elevated by the platform above a sea of growing hostility, I looked out from the piano and scanned the grim faces of more than 7,000 teens. I was scared. *God, if I ever needed you, it's now.*

Half of the kids were swaying in semi-drunken stupors, holding up their lighters, dulled to the words I sang by the liquor that clouded their minds. The other half were restless and growing more out of control by the moment. A few of them began to boo at me. I took a deep breath and once again started singing "Emily."

> *You, going through this stage.*
> *It's a restless age*
> *Young and insecure.*

I've heard that during a crisis, all of your senses become sharper. Maybe that's how I recognized the Budweiser logo on the full, open can of beer that rocketed toward me. I shifted just in time to avoid a concussion, but the full force of it exploded against my shoulder. Startled, I stumbled back a step and struggled to regain my composure.

It's almost impossible to describe the emotional battle that raged inside of me at that moment. Drenched in beer, with both fists clenched, I was tempted to find the punk who had hit me and rearrange his face. But I've never been a quitter. If I stopped singing "Emily," they would have beaten me.

Added to that was the fear factor. I remember thinking that if I tried to finish the song, all hell might break loose, and somebody could really get hurt. Mostly, though, I was just confused, and I didn't have much time to make a decision. So I made one — and regretted it almost immediately.

"You guys wanna hear something *up*, huh?" I shouted with attitude. "I'll give you something *up!*" I started pounding out "Love Crusade," and soon the whole place was getting behind me for the first time. I played off the energy of the applause and went right into "Place in This World," the number one song on the local radio station. The kids went wild, cheering and singing every word.

> It was a new experience for me to be booed and disliked, and I wasn't handling it very well.

Still, even as I sang, I became angrier — only not at the crowd anymore. The teens were so smashed most of them didn't even know what they were doing. I was mad at the situation. It was a new experience for me to be booed and disliked, and I wasn't handling it very well. I was used to performing for people who appreciated what I do. I was shocked to run up against the spiritual deadness and brooding contempt of these kids.

More than anything, though, I was mad at myself. I felt defeated because I gave in to them. They wanted energy and I delivered instead of playing songs with the messages I thought they needed most. I knew I'd compromised myself and my reason for being there; I had wimped out. And so it was with a mixture of relief and disappointment that I finished "Place in This World" and shouted, "Thank you and God bless!"

Melinda Scruggs of Reunion Records could probably see the steam coming out of my ears when I stormed through the back curtain, charged down the stairs, and announced, "I'm outta here!" Certainly, nobody backstage would have blamed me for thundering off and never returning. I felt I had a right to be angry, and I was.

But no sooner had I walked out the door than I heard Him speak. "What do you think you're doing, Michael? Can't you see what's happening here? Was it so long ago that you were one of them—a lost, hurting kid who desperately needed someone to help you find your place in this world?"

Outside in the late-night air, with the grinding sounds of the next band pulsating through the walls, a part of "Emily" came back to me.

> *You feel alone*
> *Uninspired,*
> *Well, does it help you to*
> *Know that I believe in you?*

I had to go back inside. There was no way I was going to sing those words and not take them seriously. Someone had to believe in those kids. Someone had to love them. How many times had I sung from my heart,

Still, there are doubts to fade
Moments to be made
And one of them is yours.

This was my moment, a moment He had made for me. When it comes to God working in my life, I learned a long time ago to throw the word *coincidence* out of my vocabulary. Was it coincidence that just when "Place in This World" needed a boost, the song caught the imagination of a program director of a Top 40 radio station in Cincinnati who had been a long-time supporter of my music? I don't think so. Was it just coincidence that, based on listener response, he sent a fax to every major station in the country, telling them to jump on the song immediately? I really don't think so. It makes more sense to believe in God. None of these things were ordered by themselves.

> Somewhere along the way, I had forgotten what the real world was like.

The trip to Louisiana was simply the latest of His moves. As I re-entered the Longhorn, the darkness almost overpowered me. Somewhere along the way, I had forgotten what the real world was like.

If anything, the scene was more chaotic when I stepped back in, this time as an observer. The noise level was deafening. With the liquor flowing freely and the effects of all sorts of drugs kicking in, the crowd grew even uglier. I took it all in. I had been too sheltered, tucked safely within my protective circle of Christian friends. But something was starting to break inside of me. God began to renew a heart of compassion for the lost. From then on I decided that if God was opening a door for me, I wasn't going to waste any time making my mind up about entering it.

I heard later that things got even worse after we left that evening. A crowd of kids went totally out of control and literally threw one of the bands off the stage when they realized that the group was using sound tracks instead of playing live music. Fights broke out, and eventually the police arrived to try to restore order.

I knew even as I left the club that I had definitely turned a corner. That night I made a conscious decision to follow this new opportunity as far as God wanted it to take me. I wasn't looking for the chance to cross over from Christian music to the pop scene. I didn't see it as a way to become more famous, to sell more albums, or to add more craziness to my already impossible schedule.

Being in the mainstream has connected me with people who may not have a clue about who God really is. Releasing my songs to the pop market has helped me reach listeners I'd never reach otherwise.

It's Time to Be Bold

Reading through the Gospels, I am impressed that what Jesus' eyes saw, His heart felt. And what His heart felt, His hand touched. He was so much a part of His world. He hung out with some pretty unreligious characters, simply because He loved them.

Taking my music into the world was one of the best things that could have happened to my faith. You can imagine what it was like for me to suddenly be on the same label as Guns 'n Roses, working alongside celebrities who would never darken the door of a church, who invoked the "F" word with every other breath. I was overdue for a culture shock, and it's been good for me. I was getting complacent in my religious subculture, where my doctor, neighbors, managers, and most of my friends were Christians.

Many of the mainstream entertainers I meet are skeptical of religion. They've seen too much hypocrisy. And that makes me aware of how important it is for me to live out what I believe. I knew they would be watching me for a while—to see if I was for real. From Camp David to the White House, from the *Tonight Show* to *Entertainment Tonight,* from the Grammys to other high-profile events, the opportunities to share my faith have been equally challenging and exciting.

While God has been opening doors for me to the outside, He has also been doing wonderful things to strengthen me on the inside. One of those things is my friendship with Billy Graham. I deeply love that man. He and Ruth have been a profound encouragement to both my wife, Deb, and me. Not a visit passes that they don't pray with us and for us.

I am honored and humbled to be part of his crusades. It was the summer of 1994 when he invited dcTalk and me to perform at Cleveland Stadium in front of 73,000 people. This was a first, and some of his staff were a little nervous. (I can totally understand why!) It was an incredible experience. I couldn't believe that I was getting to be a part of an event of this magnitude.

The concert that night was one I will never forget. The response was overwhelming. I don't think I've ever heard Billy more focused on his message to kids. As thousands poured forward to the stage at his invitation, I remember looking over at my friend Toby in disbelief. All I could do was cry. I sat there thinking, *This is what it is all about.*

Another thing that had a huge impact on me happened at my own house about a year ago. We were having a worship time in the "great room" at our home, and members of a band called Limit-X were telling powerful stories about what God was doing in Uganda. As I listened, I began to think about the upcoming *I'll Lead You Home* tour. My imagination kicked in, and I was caught up in a vision of how I might share Christ in a concert. All of a sudden I heard a voice in my heart saying, "It's time to be bold, Michael. It's time to be bold." I saw people coming to Christ and prodigals coming home. Startled by something, I snapped out of my vision, but I couldn't help wondering, "Lord, was that you?" I finally dismissed the incident as the musings of an overactive imagination. Maybe I'd return to that sweet daydream at another time.

Some twenty minutes later, as we were getting ready to close, one of the guys in Limit-X had one more thing to share. He looked right into my eyes and said, "Michael, there's something I feel I'm supposed to tell you."

Not having known him for long and wondering why he looked so serious, I replied, "Sure, what is it?" In retrospect, I should have been prepared for his message, but I wasn't.

"I'm supposed to tell you: It's time to be bold."

I was dumbstruck. I could hardly talk, but I managed, "You wouldn't believe what that means to me. I can't believe you said that. We gotta talk."

God has used all of these experiences (the nightclub in Louisiana, my adventures with Billy Graham, and the vision He gave me in my own home) and many more to get my attention. Because I know He's been calling me out of my personal comfort zone, I've made two important decisions. First of all, I want to do everything possible to reach out to people the way Jesus did—by being in their world. I think I've always known that the medium of music is the best way for me to do that.

Second, I am convinced that I'm not the only one who is supposed to hear God's challenge: "It's time to be bold." I can't shake the notion that if believers everywhere could just be encouraged to live out their faith in the real world, then we might see a new revolution of love that will change people's lives everywhere for God. Part of writing this book is my hope of encouraging you to live out your faith boldly in the world. I'm here to rally the troops.

The following pages are filled with ideas to provoke you to think about who you are and who you can become. In them, I've tried to be as vulnerable as I can be. I've given you permission to walk around inside my life even as you allow me to speak into yours.

> . . . I'm only comfortable asking you to follow me as I follow the One who holds it all together.

Of all the things that I've learned since I wrote *Old Enough to Know*, two stand out to me as I begin this book. One is that many people take to heart what they read and try to line their lives up with the opinions of the author. After all the letters we received in response to the first book, I am awed by this phenomenon; it's a responsibility that I don't take lightly. The other is that I'm only comfortable asking you to follow me as I follow the One who holds it all together.

I'm not a scholar or a professional theologian. But I am an observer. The way I see it, only one man has ever been able to live the Christian life without making a mess of it, and He was a carpenter who grew up in an obscure village in northern Israel. From my boyhood in West Virginia through my early lean years in Nashville, I have observed Him. You can be sure that any good advice you're about to read from me, I first learned from watching His life or the lives of people He has touched. In fact, each of the following chapters grew out of something important He has shown me about how to live on the front lines with my faith.

Mostly, this is a book about love: His love for us, our love for each other, and our love for everyone who doesn't know

Him yet. Just as I was beginning to get comfortable in my faith, God reminded me of all those people who are struggling to live in the real world without His help. It *is* time to be bold—in our love for Him and for each other. There's not a doubt in my mind that God will do awesome things if we only step out to really live for Him. The words I sing in "Live the Life" are absolutely true:

There's something beautiful and bold
The power of a million human souls
Come together as one
And each in turn goes out to lead
Another by his word, his love, his deed
Now the circle is done
It all comes back to One
For it is He, and He alone
Who has lived the only perfect life we've known

For the world to know the Truth
There could be no greater proof
Than to live the life, live the life
Be a light for all to see
Every act of love will set you free[2]

It's time to be bold by living the life that God offers us through His Son, Jesus Christ.

1.

I'll Lead You Home

1
I'll Lead You Home
Getting Along with the "FAM"

*"If your faith doesn't work at home, don't
export it."*
—Howard Hendricks

If you had looked in my Nashville apartment
window that night in September of 1979, you
would have thought I was in the middle of a
nervous breakdown. Sprawled out on the
kitchen floor for three hours, I had completely
lost it. I'd hit the wall emotionally and spiritually. I was empty and confused, and had
never felt so alone. Literally shaking with
despair, I cried out for help. And God showed
up in my kitchen. He brought healing and
hope, and I haven't been the same since. He
is the best thing that's ever happened to me.
And thanks to Him, the next best thing was
just a year and a half around the corner.

After spending most of a year being nur-
tured back to spiritual health and playing
keyboards for the group Higher Ground, I
signed my first songwriting contract with Para-
gon/Benson Publishing Company. I thought
I'd died and gone to heaven. I was knocking

13

down $200 a week to do something that I loved. Writing songs for a living meant I didn't have to wait tables anymore, or work at Coca-Cola, or plant shrubs with a landscaping company.

I thought my life had peaked and God didn't have to do anything else for me. I wasn't looking for a record deal, a higher salary, or even a girlfriend—and especially not a wife. Writing music, I was as content as I'd ever been, and I labored at it sixteen hours a day. Then one afternoon while I was working in my office, Deborah Kay Davis walked by.

I thought she was the most beautiful woman I had ever seen. When she passed by, it was all over for me. I was blown away. Totally head over heels in love. I frantically picked up the phone and called my mother in West Virginia.

"Mom, I can't believe it. You're not going to believe this, Mom. I just saw the girl I'm going to marry."

"What's her name?"

"I don't know, Mom. I haven't met her yet. But I gotta go. I'll find out and call you back."

My poor mother! She must have thought I'd lost my mind. But I'd never been so clearheaded in my life.

I left my office and went searching for this girl in the warehouse. Sherlock Holmes couldn't have done a better job of tracking her down, and eventually I found myself standing outside the ladies' restroom, waiting for her to emerge. She walked out. I introduced myself. We were engaged three and a half weeks later—and married four months after that!

If we had believed the doctors who told my wife that she'd never be able to have children because of her anorexia as a teen, then the third best thing that ever happened to me would not have. Not long after we married, Debbie and I went to our pastor for advice. He gathered the elders of the church around us and prayed for a miracle: If it was God's will, He would allow us to have a child. Do we believe in miracles? We have five of them.

I love being a husband and a father. It's harder than I ever knew it would be, and sometimes I fail at both roles. Yet I can tell you one thing for sure: There is nothing more important to me than my family. I probably get my extraordinary love for my wife and kids from my mother. She knew very little about healthy family relationships as a child. At age seven, she was abandoned (along with her brother and two sisters) on a neighbor's doorstep. Separated from one another for seven years, each child lived with a different relative.

Finally, when Mom was fourteen, all four kids were reunited with their father, who moved the whole tribe to West Virginia. I'm sure that somewhere in the process of being shifted around, my mother made a decision that when her time to marry and raise children came, one motto would describe her life: *Family rules!* I feel the same way.

> Entertainment is what I do for a living; family is what I am.

It seems to me that when two people decide to have children, they make another decision as well: to spend time with those children. I get a little frustrated when people talk to me about my "music ministry." Music is not my ministry. Don't get me wrong. God has used the music to touch people's lives. Music, though, is primarily my vocation. My ministry is driving my kids to school in the morning, reading books to them while they sit on my lap by the fireplace, listening to their prayers at bedtime, and taking their mother on dates. Being a husband, a father, and a friend is my ministry. Entertainment is what I do for a living; "family" is what I am.

That's why I try very hard to keep my career from overshadowing my time with Deb and the kids. We try to go on vactions together, far from phones and fax machines. I love taking my girls on "dates" and spending one-on-one time with my boys. When I see how God is making each of my kids into a unique individual, I'm just blown away.

Creativity is important to me as a musician. I often feel a kind of spiritual rush when the idea for a new song drives me to the keyboards. But a deeper sense of accomplishment, and oneness with God, wells up within me when I really focus my attention on my children. Maybe we come closest of all to knowing our Creator God when He works through us to create a new life. There's nothing more important than family.

Away from Home, Alone

One incident that underscores the importance of my family happened on a family vacation, when Whitney, our oldest daughter, was five years old. It's still difficult for me to tell this story, but it made me appreciate the gut-wrenching anxiety that Mary and Joseph felt when they left their son behind on a return trip to Galilee. Our "Galilee" was a beach house in Destin, Florida. We were vacationing with my brother-in-law, his wife and four children, and Deb's parents and grandparents.

Driving two vans crammed full of kids, we had just returned from a little carnival fifteen minutes down the highway. After everybody piled out and rumbled up to the house, someone yelled, "Let's go down to the beach and catch some crabs!" A few minutes later, armed with my tiny net and trying to keep track of a half dozen crab-catching kids by the seashore, I looked around and realized that one was missing.

"You guys . . . anybody seen Whitney?" I shouted, not very worried because she was known to crash pretty early.

"She must have gone to bed," my brother-in-law offered, but I wasn't satisfied. I walked briskly back to the house and found her bed empty. Trying not to betray my anxiety, I told Deb. Together, we searched the grounds immediately but with no success. Whitney was not in the house. She was not on the beach. Whitney was lost.

"She rode back in your van, didn't she?" Deb asked her sister, the panic rising. "No, we thought she was with you," came the awful reply.

Unless you've experienced it, there's no way to understand the fear that parents feel when they discover that a child is lost. The light quiver in your stomach gives way to a hardened knot deep inside, and your whole central nervous system goes on alert.

There are probably two common fears that make a play for your mind during a crisis like ours. One is a paralyzing fear that renders you useless and almost comatose. The other is an energizing fear with its adrenaline rush that throws you headlong into the search. Ours was the second kind.

Calculating that we'd left Whitney back at the carnival at least forty-five minutes earlier, Deb and I bolted to the van. An instant later we were hurtling down the highway. Finding it almost impossible to give serious attention to anything except finding my daughter, stop lights and speed limits became the enemy and prayer our only weapon.

"Please forgive us, God!" I cried, burying the accelerator. "I can't believe we left our little girl."

"We trust You, Lord," Debbie prayed. "Protect her and may Your peace reign in her heart right now. Lord, please let us find her. Let her be there."

My mind was racing faster than our van, anticipating the worst, but hoping for the best. Has she been kidnapped? Has some pervert picked her up? Is she alive? An eternity later, we squealed to a stop in the carnival parking lot. No sooner had I opened the van door than a man appeared.

"Are you looking for a little girl?" he asked.

My heart was in my throat. "Yes!" I stammered.

He pointed to a gift shop and said, "She's right over there." I ran toward the tiny building, not knowing what condition I'd find her in. You can imagine my relief when I spotted my little blonde princess contentedly licking a grape snow cone.

She was in the company of a gift shop attendant who had found her, known enough about kids to buy her a treat, and reassured her with the words, "Your mom and dad will be right back for you." Then he settled in to wait for us to recognize our loss and return.

Deb and I snatched our daughter up and began to cry and hug her. After I thanked the kind man (one of the angels God assigned to watch over my family?), I bent down and took a closer look at Whitney. Was she really all right? Or was there some deep, emotional damage from being left behind? Whitney doesn't talk much, so she just crinkled up her grape-stained face and gave me that "What are you guys so excited about?" look.

Debbie held Whitney in her arms all the way back to the beach. With tears streaming down my face, I found that delirious joy makes it almost as hard to drive as heart-rending fear. When we arrived at the house, I took my five-year-old aside and said, "Okay, Whit. When we go inside, everybody's going to act a little crazy because they love you so much, and they're happy that you're not lost anymore."

Then we went in and her relatives made a big deal over her safe return. And what did Whitney do? She stood there with her thumb in her mouth, wondering what all the commotion was for and probably wishing she could trade all the hugs and kisses for another grape snow cone.

I was so deeply moved that I could hardly speak. But I felt I had to do something. So I picked Whitney up and sat her on the kitchen counter. I got on my knees and put my head on her lap, just content to be near the one God had restored to us. Maybe we love better what we've almost lost. Just then, Deb's grandfather (A. V. Washburn to the rest of the world, but affectionately known as Boom-Pop to us) said, "I think we need to thank the Lord." We all bowed our heads immediately.

"Lord, how we thank you for answering our prayers today . . ."

As he continued his prayer, choked up with emotion, tiny puddles of tears began to form all over the family room. It was a precious moment that I know I will never forget. There is nothing more important than family.

> When my daughter was lost, she was all I could think about. God feels that same way about you and me.

The View from the Father's Throne

After the crisis with Whitney, I think I understand Psalm 103:13 better. "As a father has compassion on his children, so the Lord has compassion on those who fear him." When my daughter was lost, she was all I could think about. God feels that same way about you and me.

Maybe I have a new feel for the Father's side of the cross now. It used to be that when I thought about the Crucifixion, I pictured Jesus, beaten, bloodied, and nailed to a tree. But where was God the Father when His Son was being crucified? If He was looking on from heaven, you can be sure that He had white knuckles from gripping the arms of His throne.

The day before His death, Jesus told His closest friends that He would be murdered and that each one of them would betray Him. Of course, they denied it and pledged Him their loyalty. Jesus knew better and simply replied, "Yet I [will not be] alone . . . for my Father [will be] with me" (John 16:32). But the very next day, hanging for six hours between heaven and hell, He realized something that had never happened before. Because He took our sins upon Himself, it looked like His Father had turned away from Him. "My God, my God, why have you forsaken me?" (Matt. 27:46). Those words must have pierced God's heart like cold steel.

Now if I was willing to sacrifice anything to rescue my Whitney, what must God the Father have felt on the dark afternoon His Son was crucified? I guess the more basic question is, why did He even allow it? It must be that He would do anything to bring us into His family. He turned away from His Son because He wouldn't turn away from us. He loves us that much.

Chances are, you're going through some struggles that might be keeping you from understanding His love for you. Maybe I can help to "lead you home."

Live the Life

Learn how to forgive each other. "Watch out that no bitterness takes root among you, for as it springs up it causes deep trouble, hurting many . . ." (Heb. 12:15 TLB).

A strong family is usually made up of good forgivers. We've probably done more damage by giving in to bitterness than all the other family problems put together have caused. Most of us know how it feels to be betrayed, but we don't know much about how to forgive. Maybe it's too easy to forget the times we've needed someone to forgive us.

I think Mark Twain was right when he said, "Heaven goes by favor. If it went by merit, you would stay out and your dog would go in." None of us deserves His love. He just loves us because He does.

Besides, blaming someone else for our unhappiness is such an incredible waste of time. The only thing that blame ever accomplished in my life was to take the attention off me when I was looking for a reason to explain my own depression. I'd have been better off dealing with me.

Blaming parents for your looks, brothers and sisters for your sadness, and friends for your loneliness is a worthless dead end. Forgiving them all could be the first step in finding real peace with yourself. I'll never forget the story of a young guy who left home after a huge fight with his parents in his junior year of high school.

Months later he felt awful about the things he'd done and decided to forgive his parents for the angry words they'd spoken to him. But he still had a problem. Even though he'd forgiven them, he was pretty sure they would never let him come home.

Too ashamed to ask their forgiveness in person, he wrote a letter and apologized. He told them he would be driving by the house some time on Saturday and if they would forgive him and he could return, they should hang the blue sheet from his bed on the clothesline as a sign.

That Friday night, his mother went to her laundry room and began a labor of love. When Saturday afternoon came, the boy drove past, wondering what their answer was. What he saw was every sheet in the housed dyed blue and hanging from the clothesline! That is exactly how God feels about us and the way we should treat each other.

Don't be afraid to express your love to each other. "The only thing that counts is faith expressing itself through love" (Gal. 5:6).

In "Give It Away," I sing the words:

> A *father lived in silence, saw his son become a man.*
> *There was a distance felt between them*
> *'Cause he could not understand*
> *That love isn't love 'til you give it away.*[1]

Between family members, there is no monster like silence. It grows even faster than your kids, filling first a heart, then a home, and then a family history. That's why we voice our love for one another a lot at our house. No one should have to make it through a whole day without hearing that he or she is loved.

I know you can say "I love you" so often that you cheapen its meaning, but from my experience, saying it too little is the more common problem. I think that if we discovered we had only five minutes left to say all we wanted to say, every phone line in America would be jammed with people calling members of their families to tell them of their love.

"Give It Away" continues with the lyrics,

> We *can entertain compassion for a world in need of care,*
> *But the road of good intentions doesn't lead anywhere.*
> *'Cause love isn't love 'til you give it away,*
> *You got to give it away.*

So enough with good intentions. Today tell those in your home who need to hear it that you love them. Be generous in expressing your love to others because it is the one treasure that multiplies by division. Give it away, splash it all over, empty your pockets, and tomorrow you'll have more than ever.

Don't take yourself too seriously. "The joy of the Lord is your strength" (Neh. 8:10).

Solomon showed his wisdom when he said, "I commend the enjoyment of life" (Eccles. 8:15). Satan may tremble when we pray, but I think he takes off when we laugh at ourselves. I remember the time my sister, Kim, and I drove back to Nashville from West Virginia in stony silence. We'd had an argument over something stupid, and our anger grew with each passing mile.

It's not my way to keep my emotions bottled up for long, so eventually my frustration got the best of me. I picked up my half-filled can of Coke and, with an attitude, tried to throw it out my window. Instead, the misguided can glanced off the window frame and the syrupy pop exploded all over me, Kim, and the inside of her car.

We immediately glared at each other, thought about the situation for a second, and burst into laughter. The enemy was gone. We were friends again.

The next time you're tempted to take yourself too seriously, consider my seven-year-old friend, Ashley, who suffers from aplastic anemia. If she catches a cold, it could prove fatal. Instead of choosing a trip to Disney World through the Make-a-Wish Foundation, she asked to spend a day with me. She stole my heart the moment I saw her shyly following her two lively brothers through my front door. Her curly hair and pudgy face framed the most radiant smile I'd ever seen.

Later that afternoon, with her clutching my arm as we rode through the barn on my four-wheeler, I made a resolution. Whenever I started to feel sorry for myself, I would try to remember Ashley. You'd be wise to do the same, and remember: Every time you consciously laugh in the face of trouble, every chance you have to think about the good things in your life, you bring the smiles of children like Ashley back to earth to warm us for a while.

Get back to the basics. "Whom have I in heaven but you? And earth has nothing I desire besides you" (Ps. 73:25).

In the movie *City Slickers*, a tough but wise old wrangler named Curly gave citified Mitch some hard-earned advice:

"You city slickers, none of you get it," accused Curly. "Do you know what the secret to life is?" he drawled.

"No, what?" asked Mitch.

"This," replied the cowboy, raising one finger in the air. "One thing. Just one thing. You stick to that, and everything else don't mean manure."

"That's great," said Mitch. "But what's the one thing?"

Curly measured the thirty-nine-year-old cowboy wanna-be and replied, "That's what you gotta figure out."

A key word in getting back to basics is *simplify*. With a schedule like mine, I could get caught up in the whirlwind pace that jet-setters keep, but it would be the end of me. You see, Mitch might not have figured out what that one thing is yet, but I have. It's loving God first, and then taking care of my family and friends. Maybe it's time for you to concentrate on just one thing yourself.

Recommit yourself to caring for one another. "Above all, love each other deeply, because love covers over a multitude of sins" (1 Pet. 4:8).

I suppose being taken for granted could be a kind of backhanded compliment. It probably means that someone feels comfortable enough around you that sometimes they forget you're there. But recently I've been trying to practice an attitude of gratitude for those I love — especially my wife.

Debbie is my best friend, a great mom to our kids, and the perfect mate for me. She's easygoing and laid-back, while sometimes getting me to sit still is like trying to nail Jell-O to a tree. She's one of the least materialistic people I've ever met. Soon after her graduation from Wheaton College, she opened a nutrition clinic for a poor neighborhood in Haiti, living there for almost a year. She could live in a shack and be content. I admire her for that.

Deb doesn't need much, but I need her. I'm in love with her not only romantically, but spiritually as well. Having loved Jesus since childhood, she's deeply sincere about her faith and has been a steady inspiration to me.

In fact, I'm thinking of her when I sing "The Other Side of Me":

> *If they were to write about*
> *The story of my life,*
> *They would have to mention you*
> *With every page they'd write. . . .*
> *Always love me—Never leave me now.*
> *Now you are the other side of me.*[2]

I've observed Debbie through the years and have decided that no one has a tougher job than a mother. Men want to improve the world. Mothers want to improve the whole family. Fathers teach us what we should become. But mothers teach us who we are. Deb has taught me that "I" doesn't have to be capitalized. Always concerned about others, she's a living love letter directly from God to me. Who she is reminds me that being a husband, a father, and a friend is not my job; it's my life.

> Fathers teach us what we should become. But mothers teach us who we are.

In many ways, our family is no different from yours. We have problems and heartaches just like everyone else. But we're learning how to forgive, how to laugh at ourselves, and how to get back to the basics. And most of all, we're learning that no matter what happens, we're committed to caring for each other.

I believe it's what goes on inside the walls of your home that determines how much you're going to influence people on the outside. If you want to be serious about being bold and living out your faith in the world, home is the best place to start.

- If you want to be serious about
- being bold and living out your
- faith in the world, home is the
- best place to start.

2.

You'll Never Make It Alone

2
You'll Never Make It Alone

The Importance of Christian Friends

"The meeting of two personalities is like the
contact of two chemical substances: if there is
any reaction, both are transformed."
—C. G. Jung

Even though I'd signed up to go on a men's
retreat with some of the guys from my home
church, I decided at the last minute not to
attend. What with trying to mix the new album and all, I barely had time to breathe. So
I made up my mind: I'm not going, and that's
that. Then the phone rang. I must have felt
guilty because I knew who was calling. I let it
ring twice before I picked it up. I'm not even
sure he said anything before I exclaimed,
"Finto . . ."

"Michael W.," he cut in. "Don't you even
think of backing out on this retreat. I'm picking you up in one hour."

It's hard to stay mad at Finto for long. He's
not charismatic like a movie star but he's got
the servant's heart of Mother Teresa, the bold
spirit of the apostle Paul, and the greatest gift
of encouragement of anyone I know. Other
than my father, he has had more impact on

me than any man alive. And so I surrendered willingly to a four-hour drive into the mountains with him. There was no longer any doubt in my mind that I was supposed to be on this retreat, and we weren't far down the road before I was pouring out my heart.

"Finto, do you ever wish there were two of you? I mean, sometimes I think I'm going to be pulled apart by all the responsibilities. Everybody wants a piece of me, and I'm getting close to losing it. Something's got to give because there's definitely too much pressure. And you know as well as I do that this is not the way it's supposed to be."

Finto is a passionate, in-your-face type of listener. He's always poured his life into me. After he was sure I'd gotten it all out, he let me have it with his characteristic bluntness.

> It's not the number of hours that are wrong, it's what we are filling those hours with.

"Michael, don't be so discouraged. I made the mistake of complaining about this very same thing once to a missionary wife. She looked me straight in the eye and said, 'There are twenty-four hours in a day. That's what God put there. It's the same twenty-four hours that Abraham had, and Paul, and Jesus. It's not the number of hours that are wrong, it's what we are filling those hours with.'"

Finto continued, "There are so many hours in the day that we fill with things that are of little importance to the Creator. He never has more for us to do than there is time for. We have to determine exactly what is of God and . . . what is not of God. You must make a deliberate choice."

Of course he was right, and I knew it. See, I've learned the hard way to choose the kind of friends who will lift me up and give me a clear perspective on life.

I became a Christian when I was ten, and for a long time I was "on fire" for God. The Jesus Movement was sweeping across America, and I wore a big wooden cross and carried a Scofield Bible. Even in our little town of 5,000, we had a youth choir of seventy-five to eighty kids. Most of my Christian friends were older than I was, and we'd make the rounds to each other's houses for prayer sessions where we'd sing and worship God. It provided a great support system for my new faith.

Later in high school, though, after most of those friends had gone off to college or gotten married, I started to believe the lie that I'd been missing out on all the fun. Sometimes you hang out with the wrong kind of people because it seems there's no one else to hang out with. Eventually you're deep into the party scene. Then before you know it, you're experimenting with stuff that could kill you, and life gets too crazy for words. That was my story.

Now I look back on those years and realize the importance of having Christian friends. At just the right time, God brought Don Finto into my life. He loves me enough to deflate me when he sees the need for it and builds me up when I'm down. He once told me that God took the first forty years of Moses' life to prove to him that he was somebody (in Pharaoh's household). Then He spent the next forty years (on the backside of the desert) showing him that he was nobody. Finally, in Moses' last forty years, God showed the world what He could do with somebody who knew he was nobody.

Now and then I'll call Don just to hear the firm exhortation he's spoken so may times: "He's got His hand on you, Michael. It's only by the grace of God . . ."

Just being around Finto makes me want to be more of a godly man. I want that glow he has. You can't miss it. He walks into a room and his face just radiates the love of Christ. That's where I want to be, and I don't want to wait until I'm sixty-five years old to get there. Which is probably why God put another special friend in my life. I call him Guido. He's the most radical Christian I've ever met; he's constantly challenging my faith and holding me accountable.

One day, Guido locked onto me with that intense spiritual radar of his and said, "Don't believe what people are saying about you, good or bad. They'll either underestimate you or overinflate you." Then, with a warm smile, he did laser surgery on my ego. Holding up a Bible, he said, "Here is your best critic, Smitty. Your worth is not what others think of you. What's important is what He thinks of you."

> Your worth is not what others think of you. What's important is what He thinks of you.

Guido's taught me a lot about true spirituality, and I'm convinced that there's nothing he wouldn't do for God. Still, it's probably his humanity that I love most about him. After all, no one needs a friend who can't understand your problems because he has none of his own. This truth became real to me recently when we agreed to meet at a gymnasium for a workout.

I got to the gym late and found Guido already on the Stairmaster with his eyes closed. My first impression was, "Guido's praying; I'm not gonna bother him." Just as I turned to climb onto the next Stairmaster . . . there she was.

We chose 5 P.M. on a Saturday to exercise because we assumed there would be no one there to distract us. But the girl on the stationary bike in front of me was more than I could deal with. I am deeply in love with my wife and will always be a one-woman man. Still, for some reason, on that particular night, this girl's striking beauty caught me off guard, and I found myself struggling not to look at her.

"Man, I sure wish I could talk to Guido," I thought. But

one glance in his direction told me that he was even deeper into his prayer than before. So I threw myself into the workout with an enthusiasm that would have surprised him if he'd seen me. I was sweating my brains out, and not all because of the Nautilus machines. To make matters worse, it seemed that she appeared at every station I chose to use.

Of course, each time I looked at Guido, I saw a man who appeared to be in a dimension totally separate from the one where I was doing battle. With his eyes closed and his lips moving in silent prayer at the same furious pace as his driving legs, he was turning that Stairmaster into a staircase right up to heaven. I admired him, but it didn't help me feel any better about myself. He was obviously more spiritual than I was, and I decided to keep my thoughts private. Finally, the workout ended.

One of the great things about having true friends is that you can be yourself with them, and they'll still love you. Walking out of the gym together later, I couldn't hide my feelings any longer.

"Bro, I gotta confess," I blurted out.

"What's up?"

"While we were in there working out, I was struggling to keep my eyes off that girl in the exercise room. I want to confess my sin and ask you to speak forgiveness to me."

I felt better immediately. I had no idea what his response would be, but the one I got was completely unexpected.

Guido's eyes grew as big as saucers and he started laughing hysterically. "Bro, I can't believe it!" he cried. "I thought I was the only one fighting it. Why do you think I was praying through the whole workout?!"

"Admit your faults to one another," said James, "and pray for each other so that you may be healed" (James 5:16 TLB). After confessing our struggles, we prayed together and had a great time of fellowship for almost forty minutes. If I hadn't gotten rid of the guilt I was feeling, I would have carried it on with me. Instead, I came away from that experience stronger because of being honest with a close brother in Christ. There is simply no substitute for a friend who knows you well and loves you anyway.

> I've learned firsthand that success can be just as hard to deal with as failure.

I've learned firsthand that success can be just as hard to deal with as failure. Although I might not have recognized it a few years ago, I now readily admit I was enticed by the success that came when "Place In This World" became a pop hit. Suddenly I was thrown into a whole new arena where egos are indulged and pride goes unchecked. It can be very tempting to feed off applause and start believing the praise you receive from people.

But I have solid friends who can be brutally honest with me—and I've given them an open invitation to do exactly that when they think I need it. I've said to them, "When I get out of line, please knock me upside the head." Every believer needs that accountability.

Two friends who serve as my spiritual watchdogs are my managers, Mike Blanton and Dan Harrell. They remind me that I'm capable of making mistakes and encourage me when I need it. I love those guys deeply and literally trust them with my life. That's why I wasn't surprised when they arranged a time for the three of us to get together in Colorado to talk and pray about our work together and my future in particular.

The Lord knew what He was doing when He put Dan and Mike together and then placed them in my world. Dan

Harrell is the ultimate businessman, a godly man so organized and methodical that I sometimes think we came from different planets. Since I tend to be spontaneous and impulsive, I desperately need Dan's wise counsel to keep my life on track.

Mike Blanton is the visionary whose artistic sense has never failed me, a man who knows me so well that sometimes I think we share the same heart. He started the meeting off by saying, "I've got three things I want us to talk about tonight. First of all, what is your greatest fear?" I can't remember all of Mike's questions, but I'll never forget how easily we opened up to each other.

"I guess my greatest fear will always be that something bad might happen to one of my children," I said. And then we talked about our families, our highest hopes, and our worst failures. A special kind of healing and bonding happens when you admit your faults to a close friend. There we were, three business associates, but more important, three misty-eyed Christian brothers confessing our deepest fears to one another—and so turning our hearts toward the Lord.

We each revealed our struggle with the success syndrome, so it was natural for Mike to say to me, "Bro, do you realize what you've been called to do? God has opened up enormous doors for you, both in the Christian market for believers and in the mainstream. But you'll never be just a pop artist.

"He's given you a gift to encourage kids. Take a year and just listen to the Lord. Put that on the album . . . and just see what He does with it."

Having long ago earned the right to speak into my life, he added, "Your life isn't about how big and loud and unfocused we can make your next tour. God's made you an encourager for the Body everywhere. You need to use that position to speak what's on your heart."

Had I just heard God say again, "It's time to be bold?" As you may know if you've heard the album *I'll Lead You Home* or saw a concert on that tour, I tried to dig deeper to express both my struggles and my firm conviction that Christ is the hope of this world.

The View from the Cross

The man who was executed on a cross outside Jerusalem was exactly like us—and nothing like us. In Jesus, we have a friend who is able "to sympathize with our weaknesses . . . one who has been tempted in every way, just as we are" (Heb. 4:15).

When you're betrayed by someone you thought you could count on and you're not sure you'll ever be able to trust anyone again, He understands. He was first betrayed by a kiss, then denied three times.

When you stand beside the coffin of your best friend and feel that your heart is broken beyond mending, He understands. Ten of His closest companions were murdered within a few years of each other for the singular crime of believing in Him—and He watched it all happen.

Max Lucado calls Him the God who came near. "For thirty-three years He would feel everything you and I have ever felt. He felt weak. He grew weary. He was afraid of failure. He was susceptible to wooing women. He got colds, burped, and had body odor. His feelings got hurt. His feet got tired. And his head ached." He understands. He was a man. He was exactly like us.

Still, in an important way, He was nothing like us: "tempted in every way, just as we are—*yet without sin*" (Heb. 4:15, emphasis mine). You and I are a lot alike. At our best, we take a few steps forward and slip one back. Jesus is different from us. He was tempted to lie, but He told the truth. He was tempted to envy, but He chose to encourage. He was tempted to take sexual advantage of a woman, but He decided to love her instead. Jesus may have always been able to understand our weaknesses, but until He faced death, when He who knew no sin became sin for us, there was something about us that He couldn't understand—*what it felt like to be guilty.*

His life was a mixture of the mundane and the miraculous. Although He lived as a man, He was the One who came to open blind eyes, cleanse lepers, and ultimately give His life to give us eternal life. There is no greater miracle than the fact that He knows us completely and still chooses to call us His friends.

Live the Life

Another thing you and I have in common is that we both need friends. If you can think of me as one of yours, I've got some great advice for you—especially if you're

> *Wandering the road of desperate life,*
> *Aimlessly beneath a barren sky,*
> *Leave it to me,*
> *I'll lead you home.*[1]

Work on your most important friendship. There are friends who pretend to be friends, but "there is a friend who sticks closer than a brother" (Prov. 18:24).

There are some things in my life I could give up with no regrets. But one thing is non-negotiable: my friendship with Jesus Christ. The other day I was driving over to a friend's house. Suddenly, I started to feel down. *What do I have to be depressed about?* I thought. *I'm committed to the Lord. I've got a great family and friends who love me. My career's going great. I should be ecstatic!* But I wasn't.

There's nothing as depressing as being depressed for no reason. So I took personal inventory as I drove, and eventually, I felt I had an answer. Most of the goals the world sets for you simply don't satisfy when you achieve them. C. S. Lewis said, "Aim at heaven and you will get earth thrown in. Aim at earth and you get neither." I guarantee you that some of the most successful entertainers in the world are the least at peace with life. They know that *things* don't fulfill. I know that *God* does. The best answer to the question "What is life?" came from Jesus: ". . . that they may know you, the only true God, and Jesus Christ, whom you have sent" (John 17:3).

> Most of the goals the world sets for you simply don't satisfy when you achieve them.

I realized that I was depressed because I had just been going through a phase when I'd hardly had a moment to myself, rushing from one responsibility to another. I can only take the insanity of an impossible schedule for so long, and then I've got to slow down and get back to the basics. Life that pushes Him into the background is not life—and always leads to depression. Jesus knew something when He said, "So do not worry. . . . But seek first his kingdom and his righteousness, and all these things will be given to you as well" (Matt. 6:31, 33).

Like any friendship, yours with Christ will not happen overnight, even though He's more than willing. It's just that it usually takes most of us some time to finally believe that He loves us as much as He does. But His friendship is worth your time, and when you find it, you find life.

Look for friends who will hold you accountable. "As iron sharpens iron, so one man sharpens another" (Prov. 27:17).

You'll never make it alone. Whether it's your pastor, parent, friend, spouse, or roommate, give those you love permission to walk around inside you and help you get an honest picture of yourself.

Hang out consistently with at least one solid Christian friend. "Two are better than one. . . . If one falls down, his friend can help him up" (Eccles. 4:9, 10).

There's a reason Jesus sent His disciples out in pairs. You were never meant to make it alone. It's the rare believer who can hold his or her own against the predictable pressures of the people he or she hangs out with. Fifteen-year-old Wayne from British Columbia wrote with a problem common to many of us:

> My "fave" line from "Go West Young Man" is "Why must I wander like a cloud, following the crowd? Well, I don't know." It's so true, Michael. At the high school I attend, all my friends are doing drugs, drinking alcohol and smoking—every single one of them. Sometimes I feel like I'm the only kid in the world who's not into anything like that. But the pressure to conform is almost more than I can take. How much longer can I make it?

My best "guesstimate" for Wayne is *not much longer.* The wisest of men said, "He who walks with the wise grows wise, but a companion of fools suffers harm" (Prov. 13:20). It doesn't take a trained sociologist to see that for most people, the peer group is the real world—a world where your values are determined by your friends.

Every one of us needs at least one strong Christian friend like the one I sing about in "Straight to the Heart":

> *Over the years I've learned one important thing*
> *It's that real friends shall never truly be apart.*

You were there in my darkest time of need
With a hand reaching straight to the heart.[2]

You'll never make it alone. The pressure on you to con-
form to this world's standards is growing more intense by the
hour. When I was in school, the "hard stuff" meant algebra.
Now you can get about any drug you want if you know the
wrong person. When it comes to sexual pressure, things are
getting out of control. A recent survey of 900 teens by *Seven-
teen* magazine revealed that:

- More than 75 percent used birth control.

- 37 percent of the girls and 58 percent of the boys said
  there is nothing wrong with premarital intercourse and
  "I intend to try it or have done it."

- Only 22 percent of the girls and 16 percent of the boys
  said that sex before marriage was a bad idea.

Unfortunately, Christian kids aren't much different. Research shows that by the twelfth grade, 62 percent of today's
churched teens have been sexually involved.

"Though one may be overpowered," said Solomon, "two can
defend themselves" (Eccles. 4:12). Although there's nothing
wrong with having a large group of Christian friends, it's not
very realistic to think that you can always be surrounded by a
protective circle of believers. God knows that just one or two
other friends who share your faith is enough to encourage you
and help you defend yourself against the pressures you face.

Don't be afraid to reach out to others. "Keep yourselves
in God's love" (Jude 21).

Being a friend is the most natural way to influence people,
and it seems to be God's favorite strategy for reaching the
world with His love. He places a high priority on putting

friends first. I'm much more at ease now than I used to be about sharing my faith. Maybe that's one reason He's opening up so many more doors for me. I find that being a true friend is far more effective than the intimidating, pressurized style I was conditioned to in the past.

Recently I went out for lunch with a record rep who was helping me do some interviews and guest jocking for a Top 40 radio show. We'd worked hard together that day and I was enjoying getting to know him. Just before the waitress came to take our order, I remember praying, "Lord, I have no idea where this guy is spiritually or what he believes about You. Guide our conversation and, if I'm supposed to speak to him about You, open that door."

Hardly a moment had passed before my new friend said, "Listen, for some reason I feel like I have to tell you something. Maybe you could help me. I got married a few months ago and my wife wants me to change over to her religion . . ." Of course, I'm sitting there thinking, God, You really are too much! I love the way You work.

There I was, sitting in a booth across from a man I had known less than one day, and he started talking to me about spiritual things. The more I listened, the more he could tell that I genuinely cared about him, and the more he opened up to me. He talked about his wild past, and I listened without judging. In fact, his story sounded kind of familiar, and I told him so.

"Hey, I became a Christian when I was ten years old," I said to him. "But there was a time when I drifted away."

"You did?" he exclaimed, obviously surprised by my confession.

What I told him next was the most natural thing for me to say: "I can't begin to explain to you the peace that God has given me in my heart since I recommitted my life to Jesus

Christ." God was walking across the bridge of friendship He had built between us that day to meet a man who, quite possibly, had never seriously considered His love before. I think I understood at that moment why Jesus enjoyed the title sarcastically given to him by the religious leaders of His day: "a friend of tax collectors and sinners." Sinners are real people with real names, real families, and real needs. And because of His great love for them, they are often attracted to the real Jesus.

The fact is that we have a relentless, compassionate, and merciful God. It's time for us to be bold enough to show people who don't know Him that they don't have to perform to get His attention. Neither do they have to work to earn His love. He loves them exactly the way we should—*just because He loves them.*

3.

If All Else Fails,
Follow Directions

3

If All Else Fails, Follow Directions

Getting into the Word

"A really intelligent man feels what other men only know."
—*Montesquieu (1736)*

So breathe in me
I need you now
I've never felt so dead within . . .[1]

Those words describe exactly what I was going through for several months last year. I was in a major funk. A cloud of gloom hung over my life. I would go to church and sit there quietly weeping. *Where are you, Lord? I feel numb spiritually. I'm not a good father, husband, or friend. I don't do much of anything right. Why can't I snap out of this depression?* I begged God.

But very little changed for a long time. I would have a few good days, and then the cloud would settle over me again. Until finally, I'd had enough. After a particularly tough week, I woke up without an alarm at 5:30 on a Saturday morning—the only day of the week I get to sleep in. For weeks I hadn't been able to pray except to recite the Lord's Prayer. All I could get out were groanings. Early that morning, though, I drove to the studio so I could be alone and really pour out my heart to God.

"Why can't I hear you anymore? God, where are you?" I cried out. "I can't do this anymore. I desperately need to hear from you." Sitting at the piano, my prayer was not much more than a desperate jumble of thoughts.

Suddenly, I *did* hear from Him. I'm sure I heard a voice say to me, "I know you feel lost. I know you feel alone. I'm going to lead you home, son. I'm going to complete the work I began in you."

Although I had no intention of writing when I sat down at the piano, I put my hands on the keyboard and, five minutes later, I finished writing the music and chorus for "I'll Lead You Home." Isn't it interesting that after a time of depression, you realize you have relearned something that you thought you already knew? How long will it be before I finally understand just how much He loves me? How many times will I get caught again in the trap of trying to earn His love? I'm certain that this is my greatest weakness, and it all goes back to my biggest problem: unbelief.

If I really believed that He loves me as much as the Bible says, this low self-esteem thing that eats away at my faith wouldn't paralyze my growth like it does. I've always been my own worst critic. It's hard to break the pattern of beating up on myself and instead rest in His love. How good it would be if I could learn, once and for all, that God is much easier to live with than I am.

I waste too much time asking the wrong questions: Am I singing well enough? Am I writing good music? Do I look all right? Am I being a good enough husband and dad? I know what the important questions are: Am I going to let Him love me? Am I going to be more concerned with what He thinks of me or what the world thinks of me?

Fame, popularity, physical attractiveness, and other surface things that most people value don't last long—certainly not beyond the grave. It's nice to be appreciated, but if I had a choice between listening to applause or listening to God's Word, there's really no contest.

I feel for people who get their self-worth from the way they look or how well they perform. It's a no-win situation. That's why I wrote "Picture Perfect."

> *Pull all your hair up*
> *Dab on the makeup*
> *Tryin' hard to look so pristine*
> *Like a face on a magazine*
> *Those fancy dressers and media pressures*
> *But you're feelin' so plain and small*
> *If you don't look like a paper doll.*
> *Don't you know that I love you?*
> *You don't have to be picture perfect*
> *To be in my world.*
> *You don't have to be picture perfect*
> *To fit the frame.*[2]

God loves you for who you are, not for what you do or what you look like. He takes all the pressure of unrealistic expectations off you and replaces it with His unconditional acceptance. That's because God sees things very differently than we usually do. He doesn't focus on your outside very much because He's too busy helping you make the inside beautiful. "The Lord does not look at the things man looks at," God said to Samuel. "Man looks at the outward appearance, but the Lord looks at the heart" (1 Sam. 16:7).

One of my favorite paintings is of a father on his knees,

praying over his sleeping child. I honestly can't tell you what the frame around that picture looks like. It's the picture that's important to me.

God is the same way. He's given us a book to teach us how to develop our pictures

● God loves you for who you are, not for what you do or look like. ●

correctly. The best thing to do, then, is to live by what we learn there.

If all else fails, follow instructions. And take my word for it: All else will fail. Money can be lost or stolen. Popularity can leave as quickly as it comes. Age will eventually wear down the body of even the greatest athlete. The normal trials of life will destroy your pride. But what you've committed to your spirit will be yours forever.

Rendezvous at Radnor Lake

I'll never forget the day Pastor Don called and asked if I could meet him at Radnor Lake, a beautiful place to walk, just outside of Nashville. I jumped at the chance to be with him, and soon we were strolling along the trail. As we were casually walking and catching up on each other, he did something that amazes me to this day. Finto turned to me and said, "Michael, 'since the day [I] heard about you, [I] have not stopped praying for you and asking God to fill you with the knowledge of his will through all spiritual wisdom and understanding'" (Col. 1:9).

Eventually he quoted Paul's entire letter to the Colossians to me from memory. I realized finally what he was doing—and I have never been the same since.

When he finished reciting Colossians, I knew two things for sure. First, up to that moment, I'd had no idea how powerful the spoken Word of God could be. Finto calls it speaking Scripture into someone's life, and as he quoted verse after verse, it was like each of them was written directly to me. I was awestruck.

I'm used to sitting down and reading a book but this book, "living and active . . . sharper than any double-edged sword" (Heb. 4:12), was literally reading me. It probed deeply, even as it encouraged me; it penetrated "the thoughts and intentions" of my heart at the same time that it gave me hope. I learned that the "sword of the spirit" can cut *and* caress at the same time.

Second, I knew I had to devote myself to learning Scripture, both memorizing it and applying it to my life. This was no small task. English was tough for me in high school but homework that required memorization was next to impossible. However, after my experience at Radnor Lake, I was determined to store up God's Word in my heart.

The first passage I chose was Colossians 1:9–16. It took me until two o'clock in the morning to memorize it, but I was so excited that I could hardly sleep. Since that time, I've committed other lengthy parts of the Bible to memory, including the Book of Colossians and key chapters in Romans, Psalms, and Ephesians.

If there was just one thing that I could have you understand about me, it would be this: I have a consuming desire to know God. I suppose it was only a matter of time before memorizing Scripture would become an important part of my life. I had a hunger for God for years but wasn't sure how to get close to Him. I wanted to be where He was, and I discovered that even though you can't always find Him in music, in friendships, or even in religion, you can always meet Him in His Word.

I'm going through a good phase of my life right now where

I really want to know Him. I'm learning that in order to grow as a believer, there's no substitute for getting into the Word. But as I travel, I find relatively few people who are radically going after scriptural truth. A staff reporter for the *Wall Street Journal* who did an article on me a few years back wrote, "America is becoming a nation of Bible illiterates, its citizens unable to find the time or inclination to read the world's best-selling book." I agree with him.

Even though the Bible still racks up impressive sales, research shows that very few members of the more than 90 percent of U.S. households who own a Bible actually get around to cracking it open. Barna Research Group, a Glendale, California, pollster revealed that only one in ten Americans claims to be a daily reader. Among people under twenty-five, the percentage dropped to fewer than one in thirty.

If these stats are anywhere near accurate, we're in some trouble. America is always just one generation away from atheism. And if only one in thirty youth is an active Bible reader, the trouble could be deeper than we imagined. What can be done to reverse this trend? Maybe if people understood why God gave us the Word, they would better see their need for it.

The View from the Garden

It looks to me like God's original plan was to hang out with us—up close and personal. He walked with Adam and Eve in the Garden of Eden "in the cool of the day." He spoke to them face to face as someone does with a good friend. But the first man and first woman chose themselves over God and were banished from the garden, bringing their daily walks with God to an end.

God watched us moving further and further from Him, killing each other and growing more corrupt by the year. It seems we had succeeded in only one thing: grieving God's heart so that He was sorry He ever created us. It was a tough decision but a necessary one when He washed this planet clean with a mighty flood, saving only a few people to begin again.

Yet God wanted desperately to get back in touch with humankind. So He chose a righteous man named Abraham to father a remarkable nation, eventually called Israel. His plan was to use that nation to bless all other nations and show them how much He loved them. Finally, He even sent His own Son to be crucified on a cross—the ultimate proof of His love for us.

The Bible is still one of the major ways that God speaks to us today. Left to myself, I've got a good track record for getting lost. So time and again I've gone to the Word to find out God's direction for my life.

If we live by our instincts, we'll usually choose the path of least resistance and make a mess of our lives. I was proud of Ted Koppel, the host of ABC's *Nightline*, when he dropped a bomb of a controversial statement at Duke University's commencement. He declared:

> We've actually convinced ourselves that slogans will save us. Shoot up, if you must, but use a clean needle. Enjoy sex wherever and with whomever, but use a condom. *No!* The answer is *no.* Not because it isn't cool, or smart, or because you might end up in jail, or dying in an AIDS ward. But *no* because it's wrong. Because we've spent 5,000 years as a race of rational human beings trying to drag ourselves out of the primeval slime by searching for truth and moral absolutes in its purest form. Truth is not a polite tap on the shoulder. It is a howling reproach. What Moses brought down from Mt. Sinai were not the Ten Suggestions.

The Bible shows me, even more faithfully than a best friend could, exactly what I look like on the inside. No source can help me see the real me better than Scripture. In fact, the Bible calls itself a mirror (James 1:23), and you're supposed to do something about the reflection it reveals to you. I got a good look at that reflection a while back in a Nashville restaurant.

I often carry a pocket New Testament with me in case I get a few minutes to read it during the day. No sooner had I opened it to Philippians than a young guy came up and began to pour out his gratitude for what my latest album meant to him. His sincerity touched me, and as he walked away, I began to think, "You know, I'm kinda startin' to like this. A little flattery never hurt anybody."

Then I reopened my Bible, and, of course, my eyes fell immediately on Philippians 2:3: "Do nothing out of selfish ambition or vain conceit, but in humility consider others better than yourselves." Boom. I had to confess my pride, ask for forgiveness, and move on.

In "A Little Stronger Every Day," I sing,

> I'm running blind on the wheels of faith
> Moving to the beat of a heart that prays
> Hangin' on every word you said.
> I get a little stronger every day.[3]

I've never met a sincere believer who didn't want to "get a little stronger every day," but there are no shortcuts to that kind of growth. There's a price to be paid, and it seems that few Christians want to pay it. The song goes on to say,

> Ain't gonna find any help on the TV
> Or written down on the pages of People magazine.
> It takes digging a little deeper into the good book now
> For a little sacred advice.

So if you think it's time to start "digging a little deeper," but you're not finding your Bible very user-friendly, here are a few tips that may help.

Live the Life

Trust that the Bible is definitely God's Word. Give it a chance to change your life. "All Scripture is God-breathed and is useful for teaching, rebuking, correcting and training in righteousness, so that the man of God may be thoroughly equipped for every good work" (2 Tim. 3:16).

I would never feel comfortable giving you advice about how to live your life. But I'm convinced that the Bible truly speaks to us today. I often disagree with what the latest popular spokesperson for Christianity has to say. I've always been enough of a rebel to get headstrong when someone tells me what I should believe. I've never felt that way about the Bible, though. In it are real answers for people with real problems.

Josh McDowell and others have spent their lives studying and defending the reliability of the Bible as God's Word, and they can offer proofs of its integrity. I'm not a scholar; I'm an average person like you. I have occasional doubts but, bottom-line, I believe that everything important I need to know is between the pages of this book. Before I would ever make an appointment with a psychologist, I'd go to the Bible first. It's all in there.

Get into the habit of reading the Bible daily. "Give us each day our daily bread" (Luke 11:3).

I'm not as critical of apathetic Christians as some folks are. When I see them going nowhere and doing nothing for God, I don't naturally assume they've left their faith. On the contrary, I think most people love the "idea" of God, but daily Bible reading isn't a personal reality for them. It's not that they don't believe the right things either. Most Christians are solid doctrinally, but they're not getting enough daily spiritual nutrition to keep themselves alive.

In a day when many believers are fighting a losing battle with the stresses of life, Job reminds us of the one reason he didn't lose his faith or his sanity when life crashed in around him:

> I cannot perceive Him; . . . but He knows the way that I take; when He has tested me I shall come forth as gold. . . . I have treasured the words of His mouth more than my necessary food (Job 23: 8, 10, 12).

What a great thought! If we loved God's Word as much as we love food, think of the great things He could do in our lives.

Select one of your favorite passages of Scripture and memorize it. "I have hidden your word in my heart that I might not sin against you" (Ps. 119:11).

Many people have told me that, for them, the best part of the *Friends* tour was when I quoted Psalm 139 from stage.

> Where can I go from your Spirit?
> Where can I flee from your presence?
> If I go up to the heavens, you are there;
> if I make my bed in the depths, you are there. (vv. 7–8)

A profound hush came over the audience night after night when I spoke His Word into people's lives.

> For you created my inmost being;
> you knit me together in my mother's womb.
> I praise you because I am fearfully
> and wonderfully made. . . . (vv. 13–14)

I sensed so powerfully that God was moving throughout the audience and that His Spirit was changing lives through Scripture. In fact, one man revealed that he and his wife had decided to abort their baby until he attended that concert and heard Psalm 139. Today their child is growing more beautiful by the day.

The passages that you memorize actually become a part of you and add a depth that just wasn't there before. Then, when you face a temptation or a difficult problem, you've got a resource inside you to help you get through it.

Act on what you read. "Let us stop just saying we love people; let us really love them, and show it by our actions" (1 John 3:18, TLB).

Reading the Bible can become dry, boring, and mechanical if you're not applying what you learn to your life. Some of the most dangerous people in the church today are those who have a lot of Bible knowledge but haven't acted on what they've learned. They become self-righteous, narrow-minded, and critical of everyone who doesn't measure up to their idea of what a Christian should be. There's a powerful verse in 1 John that describes the remedy for this problem.

Someone may say, "I am a Christian; I am on my way to heaven; I belong to Christ." But if he doesn't do what Christ tells him to, he is a liar. But those who do what Christ tells them to will learn to love God more and more. (2:4, 5 TLB)

If you read and obey His words, you'll become more loving and compassionate and less judgmental. So ask God to give you a desire, not just to get into the Word, but also to live out what you find there. "Show me your faith without deeds, and I will show you my faith by what I do" (James 2:18).

Teach what you're learning to a friend. "And the things

you have heard me say in the presence of many witnesses entrust to reliable men who will also be qualified to teach others" (2 Tim. 2:2).

There's that accountability factor again. You'll be stronger if you have a friend who needs you to be strong. There is no such thing as reading the Bible for yourself. God's Word is relational. The truths you read in it will point you away from yourself to friends who need you.

Chad, a seventeen-year-old senior, wrote to me from Indiana:

Dear Michael,

Thanks for answering my letter and telling me to get into the Word and to stand up for what I believe at school. Well, guess what? I got elected co-captain of my basketball team, and another guy and I decided to start a Bible study for the players. The whole thing is voluntary. No one has to come, so I didn't think anyone would. But two weeks ago, eight players came, and last Wednesday morning, twelve guys showed up. We read some verses for a while, then we stopped and talked about it, trying to relate it to our lives. Reading the Bible has never been this exciting before. Thanks for encouraging me.

Your friend,
Chad

The Bible. Read it. Memorize it. Trust it. Believe it. Consume it. Eat it, drink it, sleep it. And watch how your life will be radically changed.

4.

A Father
Who Listens

4
A Father Who Listens
Learning to Pray

*"If you don't come apart and rest awhile,
you'll simply come apart."*
—A. W. Tozer

A half hour before the concert was to begin, Amy Grant looked discouraged to me. With her head lowered in silence, she sat alone in the corner of a large dressing room. Even though her face was covered by her hands, I knew there was a pained expression on it— at least every time she swallowed. A troublesome sore throat had bothered her for days, but on this night it was tormenting her without mercy. The grind of the *Lead Me On* tour was taking its toll on all of us. Still, I was sure that Amy, always a trooper, wouldn't even consider not performing. I wished there was something I could do.

When we got together for our usual preconcert prayer time, a thought that had been growing inside me for weeks finally took root. We were all aware that our nightly prayer ritual could become a meaningless habit, and I was determined not to let that happen for me. I'd already decided to be bolder, to step out and pray with more confidence.

As our weary group began to pray, I felt a strong compulsion from God come over me. I heard no audible command, but I was positive that He was telling me to pray for Amy's

> Maybe we pray too little because our concept of God is too small.

throat. More concerned at that moment with obeying His prompting than I was with how my actions might be perceived, I crossed the room to Amy, stood behind her, and put both of my hands on her shoulders. Then I began to pray.

When Elijah finished his prayer on Mt. Carmel, the Bible says, "Then the fire of God fell from heaven" (2 Kings 1:12). I sensed that same spiritual firepower the night I prayed for Amy. God's electricity was in the air. My hands felt hot with it, and I knew that something was happening that I'd never experienced before. "Pray for each other so that you may be healed," God wrote through James (James 5:16).

When I was done praying, I turned to walk away. Amy grabbed my hand. "What was that?" she asked, amazed. "When you laid your hands on me, I was overcome with . . . this heat coming through your hands . . . the power of God . . . like a fire."

"I was praying for a healing."

"Thanks," was all she seemed able to say, still arrested by what had just taken place. She took the stage and sang her heart out for the God who heals. As I watched her perform, I didn't feel proud; I felt obedient.

"You do not have, because you do not ask," said James (James 4:2). "Test me in this and see if I will not throw open the floodgates of heaven and pour out so much blessing that you will not have room enough for it," promised the Lord (Mal. 3:10). If we knew the power that was available to us through prayer, we wouldn't give up on it so easily. Maybe we pray too little because our concept of God is too small.

We'll Get 'Em Next Time

I was shortstop on one of the worst Little League baseball teams our town had ever seen. And that was ironic because our coach was good enough to play in the major leagues if he'd tried. He knew more about the sport than any man I'd ever met, and I shamelessly held the man up as my hero. After all, he was my dad.

You might think, given his background, that Dad would have gotten discouraged trying to teach a dozen under-achieving ten- to twelve-year-olds the finer points of America's favorite pastime. I mean, there we were with only one game left on our sixteen-game schedule, and our record was a perfect 0 and 15!

To his credit, Dad never lost his temper, never showed his disappointment, and never stopped believing in us. Because of his love for us, we were probably the happiest bunch of losers in that part of West Virginia. In our league, there was a time-honored tradition that if you won a ball game, your whole team went to the Dairy Queen to celebrate. But Dad started a new tradition. After every loss, he gathered the guys together, looked each of us in the eye, and said, "Boys, don't ever give up." Then flashing a smile, he always ended his pep talk with, "Besides, we'll get 'em next time!" After that, he promptly drove us all to the Dairy Queen to celebrate our loss.

And, of course, you guessed it: We won our final game of the season. You'd have thought we'd won the World Series the way we shouted all the way to the Dairy Queen that night—our sixteenth return trip. When I look back on those years, I never regret having played for a team with the worst record in town. My dad passed along to me that summer what he had learned from his heavenly Father. From that time I've always known that win or lose, I can always go to God because He is my Father and loves me unconditionally. When you realize how much He believes in you, even though your own belief may be small, you'll want to open your heart and talk to Him.

A Father Who Listens

Many of the letters I receive reveal just how desperate some people are to find a listening ear. Sixteen-year-old Lisa wrote from New York:

Dear Michael,

I'm writing you 'cause I feel that you are the only one who will listen to me. It's really hard living at my house. All my parents do is yell at me. I wish I could run away, but I have no place to go. I don't want to live on the streets 'cause I'm scared. All I do is cry and wish that I could die.

None of my friends want to hear my problems. They all have Christian families, so they don't understand. Every time I go to my youth pastor, he seems to be preoccupied. I'm afraid of what I'm going to do if I can't find someone to help me. I guess that's why I'm writing to you.

Thanks for being my friend,

Lisa

P.S. Please write back to me and tell me what I should do.

I answered Lisa and told her that even when people let us down, there is Someone who never will. "I will never leave you nor forsake you," says the Lord (Josh. 1:5). He is a Father who listens. "Come to me, all you who are weary and burdened, and I will give you rest" (Matt. 11:28). There is a God who really cares, and there's nothing He'd rather do than listen to you. If it's important to you, it's important to Him. I understand this truth better since a girl named Bryn entered my life.

A friend at church told me about Bryn. Twelve years old and in the final stages of leukemia, she could use some encouragement. I sent her a poster and some tapes, but I still couldn't get her off my mind. So one afternoon when I was on my way to the mall, I dialed her number on my car phone. Her mother answered and was as surprised as she was grateful that I'd called. After we talked for a while, I asked her, "Ma'am, I know Bryn is probably worn out, but I'd sure love to speak with her if I could." Her pause told me that she was considering my request. A moment later, she replied, "Just a minute, I'll see if she can talk." Hearing her mom's tentative response, I thought, *This is one very sick little girl."*

The next voice I heard was Bryn's, a raspy whisper that made me strain to hear it. The minutes passed and I could tell that she was tiring. Knowing it was time to let her go, I said, "When I get out to Colorado, I sure would like to come and see you." Then there was only one thing left to say: "I really love you, Bryn, and I'm praying for you."

I heard a cough over the phone and knew she was gathering her strength to speak again. "I love you, too, Michael," she managed to sigh, her voice beginning to fade. "Thanks for calling," she said, "and I'll pray for you too."

After we hung up, I completely lost it. I had no way of knowing that she would die two short weeks later, but something told me that I wouldn't see her until we greeted each other in heaven. As my eyes filled with tears, I realized two things: that I would never finish the errands I set out to do that day, and that there was nothing I would rather do in the whole world than listen to Bryn. As long as she could speak, and even if she couldn't, I wanted to be there for her. God feels the same way about you. You have a Father who listens.

"Cast all your anxiety on him because he cares for you" (1 Pet. 5:7).

View from a Solitary Place

Sometimes there's nothing harder for me to do than pray. I know that prayer changes things and that the enemy doesn't want things to change. So he works with all the distractions in my life to keep me from praying. There are times when I know I should pray but just can't get focused on it.

Well, I found a verse in the first chapter of Mark that intrigues me. "Very early in the morning while it was still dark, Jesus got up, left the house and went off to a solitary place, where He prayed" (v. 35). The reason I found it interesting was that I'd already noticed how often Jesus tried to get away from the crowds of people who followed Him wherever He went.

> Jesus knew that the solitary place is where a Christian finds power to live life on the cutting edge of faith.

He rarely succeeded in finding time alone during the daylight hours. So we see Him rising before dawn or staying up all night to spend time with His Father.

Jesus knew that the solitary place is where a Christian finds power to live the life God desires for us. I've learned that same lesson. I could easily be victimized by the whirl-wind pace of my own life if it weren't for the "prayer walks" that have become so important to me.

Often late in the evening, when the kids are in bed and the phone has stopped ringing, I'll get away for a walk along the road that leads to my house. Or sometimes, early in the morning, before the insanity of my daily schedule kicks in, I'll get in my car and drive through the countryside. These are the times that I seriously connect with God, telling Him everything that's on my heart, or maybe just being still and knowing that He's there.

Everyone needs a solitary place to meet with God, whether it's a desk in the corner of your basement, a rusty old swing on your back porch, or ten minutes in the shower every morning away from the phone. The solitary place prepares you for what lies ahead. On the last night of His earthly life, Jesus escaped to the garden called Gethsemane. Sweating drops of blood as He began to understand more completely the terrible price He had to pay, He got alone with the Father and prayed for each of us:

> I have given them your word and the world has hated them, for they are not of the world any more than I am of the world. My prayer is not that you take them out of the world but that you protect them from the evil one. . . . As you sent me into the world, I have sent them into the world. (John 17: 14–15, 18).

Then Jesus went out and died for the sins of the world—but not until He had first prepared Himself through prayer. His example for us is clear. As He went public to die for others, His best intention is for me to do the same—but not until I've first primed myself with His power through prayer.

If the Bible is the sword of the Spirit, then I believe that prayer is the arm that swings the sword. When you leave your solitary place to go to school or work or wherever, you'll find that prayer can prepare you to take on any problem you face.

Prayer is a "foreign language" to many people. They give up too easily on it when their words seem to bounce back at them from the ceiling, or when it doesn't appear they're getting any answers. God has taught me some things in my solitary place that may help you develop your own prayer walk.

Live the Life

Learn to pray by praying. "Do not be anxious for anything, but in everything, by prayer and . . . with thanksgiving, present your requests to God" (Phil. 4:6).

Probably the lamest excuse you could have for not praying is, "I don't know how." The truth is that if you know how to talk to a friend or how to listen to one, then you know how to pray. Even if you can't think of what to say to Him, or how to say it, the Bible says that you can still have an effective prayer life.

> . . . the Spirit helps us in our weakness. We do not know what we ought to pray for, but the Spirit himself intercedes for us with groans that words cannot express. (Rom. 8:26)

Although there are plenty of books, tapes, and seminars that can help you learn to pray, I think God's Spirit is the best teacher, and He is far more spontaneous and unpredictable than most people would like for Him to be. It's His Spirit who keeps your prayers fresh and vital, gut-honest and uncluttered by ripped-off religious clichés. What seems awkward at first will eventually become second nature and full of life.

Start your daily prayer time with praise. "Enter his gates with thanksgiving and his courts with praise" (Ps. 100:4).

Prayer is more than asking things from God. It's acknowledging who He is—the Creator, the King of kings, the Lord of lords, the merciful Father, the Keeper of our souls, and the Giver of all good gifts.

Many times during a concert, I'll become aware that something far more profound than a performance is going on. Sitting alone at the piano, I'll be singing a song like "Thy Word," and an incredible sense of worship will settle over the arena. At that moment, I realize that I am no longer the performer. I've joined with the audience, and together we are in awe of His presence. "The Lord inhabits the praises of His people," sang David. As He said He would, God comes to heal, to rescue, and to love.

I've noticed that in the Book of Acts, whenever the believers got together to pray, they started their meetings with worship. They knew to "seek first the kingdom of God" (Matt. 6:33, NKJV), praising His greatness and rejoicing in all He had done. Only after they finished worshiping Him did they come to Him with their problems and requests.

God loves to answer the prayers of those who are not full of themselves. "'This is the one I esteem: he who is humble and contrite in spirit'" (Isa. 66:2). He rushes to the aid of those who admit their need for Him. To praise Him first is to clear the path for Him to reach you.

Don't pray unless you expect an answer. "If you believe, you will receive whatever you ask for in prayer" (Matt. 21:22).

There is an important promise and warning in the first chapter of James: "If any of you lacks wisdom, he should ask God, who gives generously to all without finding fault, and it will be given to him. But when he asks, he must believe and not doubt, because he who doubts is like a wave of the sea, blown and tossed by the wind" (vv. 5–8).

Don't be discouraged when God's answer is "no." "We know that in all things God works for the good of those who love Him, who have been called according to His purpose" (Rom. 8:28).

Fifteen-year-old Kathy wrote from Texas,

Dear Michael,

Last year the worst thing that could have happened in my life did. In November, we found out that my father had cancer. I prayed that he would be healed and really believed that God would heal him. Everyone was praying for him, the church, our family, and even my dad's patients (he was a doctor).

In January, the reports were good. His doctors said they were going to do surgery to remove the last of Dad's cancer and that he would only be in I.C.U. for two days. But those two days turned into two weeks, and on Feb. 11, my father died. How could anyone ever expect me to pray or have faith in God again?

The first thing Kathy needed to know was that she was not alone in her suffering. God the Father understands something about the loss of a family member. Not only was God's heart broken when Jesus was crucified, but I think He also grieves deeply with every person who loses a loved one. "Precious in the sight of the Lord is the death of his saints" (Ps. 116:15).

Maybe more important for Kathy to understand, though, is that no real prayer from a child of God will fail to get an answer. It's just that He doesn't always give us the answer we want. As difficult as it may seem right now, I'm convinced that He always gives the answer that's best. When Jesus was about to die, He asked the Father to reconsider the Crucifixion, ending His prayer with, "Yet not my will, but yours be done" (Luke 22:42). Just as Jesus committed Himself to God, I want His will to always be done in my life.

God may say "yes," He may say "no," or, as Debbie and I have often discovered, He might respond with "wait." Regardless of what that answer is, I trust that He knows what He's doing. Someday we'll understand the reasons behind His tough decisions.

Pray for your friends who need to know Jesus. "I pray also for those who will believe" (John 17:20).

> Prayer is the single most powerful tool you have for bringing those you love into a relationship with Christ.

Apparently it is part of God's plan for prayer to be a key for reaching our friends who don't know Him yet. Prayer is the single most powerful tool you have for bringing those you love into a relationship with Christ.

"Devote yourselves to prayer," said Paul, "being watchful and thankful. And pray for us, too, that God may open a door for our message. . . . Pray that I may proclaim it clearly, as I should" (Col. 4:2–4).

I know that God can reach anyone with His love, and I pray for people all the time that others have given up on. Instead of being critical of people, pray for them. It's time to stop judging and start praying. Paul continued, "Be wise in the way you act toward outsiders; make the most of every opportunity. Let your conversation be always full of grace" (Col. 4:5–6).

This is exactly the concept behind a new youth ministry in Franklin that I have had the opportunity to be heavily involved in. A group of adults who have hearts for kids raised funds while many of the local teenagers cleaned, painted, and renovated a warehouse in a nearby business district. We brought in video screens, a serious sound and light system, top-notch DJs, and bands to perform. When we opened the doors to this dance club in April of 1994, a longtime dream of mine finally came to pass.

Even here in our community, there are many kids like the ones I get letters from. So on Thursday, Friday, and Saturday nights, Rocketown is a place for them to go. A committed volunteer staff of twenty college-aged believers is there to talk with and pray for them faithfully. The staff members are not critical or judgmental but genuinely concerned about the details of the kids' lives. They are making the most of every opportunity to interact with hundreds of teens, many of whom feel like everyone has given up on them. Their stories would break your heart. But we have seen even the hardest kids change when they discover that Christ is real *and has a very real love for them.* Many have come to know Christ personally. Some have been baptized. A few have given up their drug addictions. One young couple decided to marry and keep their unborn boy. One or two hurting kids have realized that suicide is not the answer. One young man has finally found "the family he never had growing up." They don't realize who draws them here. It is all because there have been so many in intense, fervent prayers from the beginning. Nightly, the staff members are on their knees praying two by two for half hour shifts until midnight. Prayer is making the difference.

The question I want to leave you with is this: Are you making a difference in your friends' lives by faithfully praying for them? It's a powerful way to demonstrate your love — and all it requires is a willing heart and a little discipline.

5.

Hanging Out in Holy Places

5
Hanging Out in Holy Places
The Place for Church in Your Life

"Where two or three come together in my name, there am I with them."
— *Jesus*

Very few people have ever heard of, let alone seen, one of my favorite movies. It's an obscure film that came out in the 1970s about the life of St. Francis of Assisi called *Brother Sun, Sister Moon*. In the movie, the hero, young Francesco, returned from the Crusades disillusioned with wealth and power, and seeking life's true meaning.

One Sunday morning, in the middle of a service that was a real snoozer, Francesco looked up from his pew and was struck by the contrast between the costly robes of the priest conducting the Mass and the stark poverty of the Christ-figure suspended on a crucifix above the pulpit. As the young man's eyes shifted back and forth from the expensive objects ornamenting the church to the bloodied figure of Jesus on the cross, an expression of pain and confusion grew on his face.

Dressed as a snobbish aristocrat himself and

73

seated in a privileged pew far from the poor people who huddled humbly in the back, Francesco battled the sick feeling rising within him. What was Jesus trying to say to him from the cross? With a look of panic, the boy finally cried, "No! No!" above the monotonous droning of the priest. Pulling at his too-tight collar, he took one last gaze at the crucified One, leaped to his feet, and rushed through the congregation on his way to the church's front door.

The next scene is hilarious and inspiring. Convinced that Jesus would do the same, Francesco ran from the church to his father's clothing store where he promptly began throwing high-priced garments out the second-story window to a cheering crowd of poor people in the street below. The rest of the film shows how Francesco discovered what the real church is all about: average people who love God so much that they really want to learn how to love each other.

I don't believe St. Francis of Assisi is alone in his search for truth or his discovery that the church should not be a country club for self-concerned people. I've been on a similar quest for years and feel that I'm beginning to get some answers. If you've questioned whether the church is relevant to your life, you might consider what God meant it to be.

View from the Pew

They ranged from severe-looking ex-cons and street-smart junkies to toothless old winos and pathetic vagrants. Here I was, surrounded by some of the toughest guys I'd ever seen.

Is this a wise decision? I wondered, looking around the room. *Do I really want to spend the night with these guys?*

I was there because it was our church's turn to host "Room in the Inn," a relief program for the homeless sponsored by several Nashville churches. In a plain building across from my church, I stood inside the doorway and watched all types of street people shuffle into the dining room where we were to feed them.

One man who stood out, and not just because of his enormous size, was Big Leon. He'd gone to prison for murder, served his time, and had been in Nashville for only two days. I found out that he had been a member of a gang in L.A. where a rival gang leader stabbed him in the neck. He had almost died there on the street, losing seven pints of blood. But Big Leon made it through the night and after he recovered, tracked down the guy who knifed him and blew him away with a .38 magnum. And now I was set to spend the next twelve hours with this man who was totally intimidating. While my brain was telling me not to get caught alone in the same room with him, something else inside me wanted to help him.

After our wives cooked a hot meal, some of my friends from church and I served it up to these hardened, homeless men. We found that they were as hungry for friendship as they were for the turkey and dressing. When the meal ended, the ladies left for home and we guys stayed on. The arrangement was that we were to spend a little time with them until they went to bed. Then with a 5:30 A.M. wake-up call, we were to prepare a cold breakfast and send them on their way by 6:15. But God had a better plan. The truth is that we hardly needed a wake-up call because we spent most of the night talking with each other.

An evening that had begun with my heart in my throat turned out to be one of the best of my life. In fact, because of the experience, I began to get a better understanding of what the church is supposed to be.

The Bible says that in the early church, "they devoted themselves . . . to the fellowship. . . . Selling their possessions and goods, they gave to anyone as he had need. . . . They broke bread in their homes and ate together with glad and sincere hearts" (Acts 2:42, 45–46). If you want to get to know someone, eat a meal with him and really listen to what he has to say. From sitting around a table with Leon and the guys, and later having a blast watching the Monday Night Football game together, I realized that the church is much bigger than a building or a program. No, when Jesus called us His Body, I think He meant we were supposed to do the same kinds of things He'd be doing on earth if He were still here in the flesh.

Once, in His hometown synagogue, Jesus picked up a scroll of the prophet Isaiah and, in a moment filled with intense emotion, read part of it to His critical listeners.

> The Spirit of the Lord is on me,
> because He has anointed me
> to preach good news to the poor.
> He has sent me to proclaim freedom
> for the prisoners,
> and . . . to release the oppressed. (Luke 4:18)

My overnight stay at "Room in the Inn" made me grateful for my church because we were following Christ's example—feeding the poor, sheltering the homeless, and preaching freedom to the prisoners; we were doing the same.

The best part of the whole experience happened when someone announced, "Lights out!" around 11 P.M. It's interesting how grown men become little boys again in the dark, sharing secrets and confessing fears they would never admit face-to-face or in the cold light of day. Stretched out in our sleeping bags on makeshift cots, we listened to lonely men who needed friends.

In the early hours of the morning, my friend Guido

finally broke through to Big Leon. Over the next half-hour, the shaken ex-con bared his soul. I listened to a convicted murderer weep because God's love was reaching out to him. It was a night I'll never forget.

Just released from prison, Big Leon cried out from his bunk, "I don't want to go back to L.A.! I don't want to go back to the gangs."

After the three of us prayed together, we explained to Leon that he could now say, "I'm outta here!" to his old life. It was a night to celebrate, and when we finally passed out from exhaustion, I knew that I'd been a part of something important.

No one could convince the members of the early church that there was anything more wonderful than being loved by God and then showing that love to their friends and neighbors. It took a long time for Christianity to become formal. There weren't any church buildings for almost three centuries. So how did people know where or what the church was in the days before building plans and big budgets? The answer is simple. Whenever people's needs were met by believers, especially the needs to be loved, forgiven, and accepted, that was the church.

In "Love One Another," I sing,

> *I had a dream that I was speaking*
> *With a prophet from the land of Wise,*
> *In a crowd of people from the land of troubled hearts.*
> *I said, "We've come here for answers,*
> *A solution to our world's demise."*
>
> *He said, "The journey would be long*
> *But here is where you start:*
> *Love one another, Love one another.*
> *Work it in to work it out.*
> *There could never be enough.*

Love one another, Love one another,
'Cause you know without a doubt,
You can change the world with love.[1]

The believers who loved each other back then didn't go to church, they *were* the church. They knew they were "living building-stones for God's use in building his house" (1 Pet. 2:5 TLB). That way, when their worship service or prayer meeting ended, they didn't leave the church to go home, hoping they could stay "up" spiritually until their next visit a week later. No one can make it by just visiting God.

But if you *are* the church, then you know that wherever you go (to work, to school, to the baseball field, and everywhere else), He is with you. You begin to learn how to live in Him even as He lives in you. And that's when the church becomes what He meant for it to be: a network of common people with common problems who really care for each other and want to share that same love with anyone else in need.

A survey done by Princeton University reports that "fewer than one out of five teenagers expressed a high degree of confidence in organized religion. In fact, although 71 percent of this sample admitted to church membership, two out of three youth blamed the church for not reaching out to them. Over 80 percent believed that a person could be a good Christian without attending church."

You might be one of those who are disgusted with organized religion or simply have questions about your relationship to the church. Maybe this will be some encouragement.

Live the Life

Give the church a chance. "Let us not give up meeting together, as some are in the habit of doing" (Heb. 10:25).

I believe in the church. Save your criticism for Satan, our true enemy. The church is too easy a target because it's made up of human beings. No wonder so many people are negative about it; the church is in a no-win situation. The reason is that God gave His perfect Word to an imperfect people. Some failure is inevitable. And of course, when our humanity gets in the way of the message, non-Christians (and many ex-church members) are quick to cry, "hypocrisy!" Who can argue with them? They're right, and you've heard me sing about it in "Calling Heaven."

The problem is that the church is weak because we are weak.

> What of the noble who are searching for the truth
> With truest of intentions?
> And yet they're jaded by
> hypocrisies behind cathedral walls.[2]

The problem is that the church is weak because we are weak. And God has only sinners to choose from when He fills the pews. "There is no one righteous, not even one," says the Lord (Rom. 3:10). But the very thing that makes the church weak can also make it strong again—if we stay humble and honest about our tendency to blow it. Where else on earth is there a collection of so many misfits who can come together and truly love one another in spite of their differences and failings?

If "Christ loved the church and gave himself up for her" (Eph. 5:25), I'm not about to give up on it simply because I recognize myself in the weaknesses of its members.

Meet regularly with a small group of other believers. "Carry each other's burdens, and in this way you will fulfill the law of Christ" (Gal. 6:2).

If a time machine could take me back, what an amazing trip it would be to walk into the temple in Jerusalem just as the worship service was beginning. To see God's Spirit settling on the sanctuary as thousands of voices joined to praise Him would be awesome.

Just as God worked powerfully when believers gathered back then, I know that wonderful things can still happen when believers get together now. But if your only experience with the church is sitting in a pew for an hour or so once a week, then you have a very small idea of what the church could mean to your life.

When the early church met in homes on a regular basis, there couldn't have been more than a dozen or so people involved. I think God had a good reason for that—the same one Deb and I had when we built a new addition on our house a while back. We knew we had emotional and spiritual needs that couldn't be met by a large group who knew little about us. We needed consistent contact with Christians who would love us during good times and bad, and who knew us well enough to help us be honest with ourselves and God. So after a lot of prayer, our dream to have a regular evening gathering of intimate friends became a reality.

When you're hurting, it's difficult to spill your insides to a couple hundred people. But you can open up to and, if necessary, break down in front of a small circle of fellow strugglers that you trust. I've also noticed that some people who might never enter a church building have no trouble going to a home filled with love and acceptance. It was the best way for the early church to spread and for its members to mature, and I believe it still is.

Some of my most tender moments with God happen when we come together on Saturday nights at my house. We purposely keep it as unstructured as possible so we can give God all the room He needs to work. It's not a Bible study or a prayer meeting, although we always pray and someone usually reads Scripture. But it's different every week, and I think that's good. Sometimes we share stories from our lives. Sometimes we simply laugh together over something silly; often we cry over something that's not. Sometimes we get together and eat. About the only thing that stays the same week after week is that we spend time worshiping Him—usually through singing. And then we just let God be God. Maybe it's time for you to do the same.

Find a church that believes the Bible is God's Word. "They worship me in vain; their teachings are but rules taught by men" (Matt. 15:9).

In the chorus of "How Long Will Be Too Long?" I sing,

> *The power of faith and love,*
> *Can change the stuff we're made of.*[3]

I believe those words are true, but that kind of faith comes from only one source: "Faith comes by hearing, and hearing *by the word of God*" (Rom. 10:17 NKJV, emphasis mine). And so Jesus had little patience with religious leaders who undercut the authority of the Bible. In fact, few things made Him angrier. One day, He turned on the Pharisees and scorched them with,

> You nullify the word of God for the sake of your tradition. You hypocrites! Isaiah was right when he prophesied about you: "These people honor me with their lips, but their hearts are far from me" (Matt. 15:6–8).

I know a guy who finished a Bible course under a liberal professor who taught him that the Bible was no more important than any other textbook. Afterward, the student confided, "I will never read the Bible again. I don't even know if I'm a Christian anymore, or even what a Christian is."

It's not hard to see why Jesus got so angry. He knew that faith comes by hearing the Word, so He went after those who were supposed to be teaching it. I'm just as concerned about the type of Christian leaders being produced by some of our seminaries today. Many theology students go into graduate schools with a zeal for God but come out with a lukewarm faith and a low view of the Bible. What we need are graduates who are radically committed to preaching scriptural truth and pursuing people motivated by their love for God. I don't think I've sung any message more urgent than this one in "How Long Will Be Too Long?":

> How long will we curtsy to the whims of new religion?
> How long will we water down the truth
> 'Til truth is no more?
> How long will be too long?

The truth is that it's already been too long, and you need to be getting your faith rooted in Scripture now. When you find a pastor who loves the Word of God and isn't afraid to preach it from the pulpit, that's the church you want to get involved in.

Don't let anything come between you and your Christian friends. "Make my joy complete by being like-minded, having the same love, being one in spirit and purpose" (Phil. 2:2).

I've been a peacemaker ever since I was little. I can confront when I have to, but it's never been easy for me. It hurts me when any of my friends are fighting, and I usually wish I could do something to help bring healing between them. I guess I've always had the idealistic notion that people should get along with each other—especially when they're Christians. And yet, Satan has probably done more damage to the church's image by publicizing our infighting than by all of his other strategies combined.

I know of people in the entertainment industry who would probably become Christians if they thought the church would show them as much love and compassion as they could get at a singles' bar. But the enemy has led them to believe that they could never be forgiven for their past, least of all by faultfinding members of the church who can't even live in peace with each other.

Our image should be the opposite. Paul wrote to the church at Corinth, "You ought to forgive and comfort . . . in order that Satan might not outwit us. For we are not unaware of his schemes" (2 Cor. 2:7, 11).

"Love One Another" ends with these words:

> *The people were then united,*
> *And in my dream we all agreed*
> *That we should start again*
> *And this would be our creed:*
> *Love One Another, Love One Another.*

So be quick to forgive people. The world is dying to be loved by us. I have had some wonderful experiences that have given me a lot of hope for what can be done through bold people who really love each other. There is a way to change the church's image from an exclusive club for self-concerned, divisive people. We'll explore that challenge in the next chapter.

6.

Finding Your Place
in This World

6
Finding Your Place in This World
Moving Up to the Mission Level

"Progress always involves risks. You can't steal second base and keep your foot on first."
—Frederick B. Wilcos

Swatting at a mosquito that somehow survived the blistering noonday sun, I stepped out of my canoe and found firm footing by a large banyan tree. I climbed the grassy riverbank and stood on a hill overlooking Zabala, a village in the interior of Ecuador. It was like a picture out of *National Geographic*, only I was there, taking in all the sights and sounds: crumbling cinder-block houses with pale thatched roofs and dirt floors; flea-infested dogs caked with mud from the previous night's rainstorm; the droning of the ever-present flies dive-bombing the remains of a wild pig that lay beside a rutted backwater road; sun-bleached shanties built over a foul-smelling garbage dump, overrun by rats as big as housecats.

But then there were the people—a total contrast to the poverty that surrounded them. With faces as radiant as their homes were bare, these brown-skinned people stole my heart with their laughter. At first, I wondered how they could be so happy when they owned so little. Their smiles confused me when I saw the squalor they lived in. By the time my mission trip was over, though, I realized they were happy for precisely that reason. They owned so little.

If you have seen the first *Little House on the Prairie* episode set at Christmastime, you will probably never forget how excited Laura Ingalls Wilder and her sister, Mary, got when Ma and Pa gave them each their very own tin drinking cup and a single candy cane. Both girls cried for joy when they reached deeper into their Christmas stockings and pulled out a shiny new penny. In the same way, the natives I grew to love as my own family, possessing almost nothing, were thrilled by a simple handshake, a hug, or a song.

I don't think I'm ever more outgoing than I am in Ecuador. I don't take much money with me, but I feel like I have a million dollars' worth of God's love, and everywhere I go, I get to hand it out to needy people. I experience a freedom there to open up that's hard to maintain here at home. In the States, we can be so suspicious of anyone who is happy and friendly just for friendship's sake. We usually suspect that somebody has a dark, ulterior motive for loving us. But the fresh-faced Ecuadorian children I meet in village after village are eager to be loved, so I hold nothing back.

On one of our last trips, I spent hours a day just hanging out with the Indian kids, making funny faces to get the little ones to giggle and singing songs to them, accompanied by an old village guitar. The presence of Christ was all around me. My intent was to bring His happiness to these people, and I couldn't give it out fast enough.

I noticed an interesting thing happening to my own faith as I touched people with His love. Instead of being depleted, it grew as I gave myself away. That same unique formula will work for you, just like Jesus promised:

For if you give, you will get! Your gift will return to you in full and overflowing measure, pressed down, shaken together to make room for more, and running over. Whatever measure you use to give—large or small—will be used to measure what is given back to you. (Luke 6:38, TLB)

A Child Shall Lead Them

On my first trip to Ecuador several years ago, an adorable little Quechuan Indian girl named Ximena followed me everywhere I went. Melted by her perpetual smile, I found myself getting attached to her, so I turned to Devlin Donaldson of Compassion International and asked, "Is anyone sponsoring this little girl?" Dev went to the head man of the village who shook his head. I didn't have to think twice. "From now on," I said, "she's going to be one of my 'compassion kids.'" And so began a spiritual love affair between me and the children of Ecuador.

I've never been in a place where people were so open to receiving God's love. I think there's a good reason why these Third World countries are responding to missionaries who tell them about Jesus. And it's not because they're "ignorant savages" as is sometimes portrayed. On the contrary, they are bright and often very wise. They hear God's voice when He calls because there's less noise in their lives to drown Him out.

They're not caught up in all the stuff that clutters our schedules and pushes God away. Having little of material value, many of the poor find more important things to live for. Learning to cope with suffering from an early age, they're more open to receiving help when it comes. Gavi's family taught me this truth in a remarkable way.

Little did I know when I was visiting Gavi, my other sponsored child, what God had planned for her grandmother, the matriarch of the clan. I'd learned that Gavi never knew who her father was and that her mother had deserted her at birth, leaving the helpless infant and her brother in the care of their grandmother. A wiry little woman with that trademark smile, Ester took it on herself to raise them on the handful of dollars she could earn in a year. I loved her for her courage and prayed for both Gavi and her regularly when I got back to the States.

The highlight of my return trip happened when I spotted them, along with Gavi's brother, Jorge, on a street of Guayaquil. They recognized me too, and we ran toward each other. The grandmother threw her arms around me, and we were so happy we wept without shame. Later, while I held Gavi close, I listened to Jorge interpret his grandmother's passionate words. Never taking my eyes off of Ester's glowing face, I heard a story, in Jorge's broken English, that brought the tears back to my eyes.

"Mr. Miguel. My grandmother, she says she watches you your first time here. How you care for her little Gavi. She says she knows, after you go, she must have the God who gives you so much love for her granddaughter. My grandmother, she says, you gone two weeks when she asks Jesus in her heart."

I was blown away. If I'd never returned to Ecuador, I probably wouldn't have found out about Ester's salvation. I knew as I sat in their home, reading the verses that she had marked in her new Bible, that I had, at least for another five awe-inspiring days, found my "place in this world."

View from the Mountain of God

My trips to Ecuador always remind me that I am most alive when God is using me to make a difference in someone else's life. If the church is going to change its image among non-

Christians, it will happen when its members learn to lose themselves in sacrificial service to others. The times I get into trouble myself are when I focus too much on my own problems.

God is looking for people who will look out for others. Why do you think Jesus spent three and a half years privately teaching His disciples? So that after His crucifixion they wouldn't fall away? So they could take over positions of power and prestige in the new church? I don't think so. Jesus literally poured His life into theirs so they would go out and do the same.

> It's clear then that the church has got to go into the world because that's where God is.

"As the Father has sent me, I am sending you" (John 20:21).

"Go and make disciples of all nations . . ." (Matt. 28:19).

"What I whisper in your ears, proclaim from the housetops!" (Matt. 10:27 TLB).

"Let your light shine before men . . ." (Matt. 5:16).

Jesus said, "Whoever serves me must follow me; and where I am, my servant also will be" (John 12:26). Then the Lord went out, touched the leper, and loved everyone who let Him, holding nothing back. It's clear then that the church must go into the world because that's where God is. Just as He told King David not to expect Him to live in the temple because "Heaven is my throne and the earth is my footstool" (Acts 7:49), God is likewise too big to be confined to the buildings we use for worship. I saw this idea become a reality a few summers ago.

A Nashville radio station invited me to help celebrate its seventh anniversary, so I signed on to headline a concert down at the city's riverfront. A crowd of at least 30,000 welcomed me warmly when I crossed the deck of an anchored barge to begin the concert. As I scanned the faces, I could tell there were people present from all walks of life, Christian and not. The more I sang to them, the more I knew this was the right place for me to be. Unlike the rowdy club I described in the introduction, this was an environment where I could really sense God's Spirit at work.

The thought crossed my mind that Jesus looked out once on an audience a lot like this one, and Matthew recorded his reaction:

> When he saw the crowds, he had compassion on them, because they were harassed and helpless. . . . Then he said to his disciples, "The harvest is plentiful, but the workers are few. Ask the Lord of the harvest, therefore, to send out more workers into his harvest field." (Matt. 9:36–38)

I fed off the energy of the riverfront concert the whole next day. And for days after that I couldn't shake the feeling that God wanted me to have more experiences like it. He had pierced the darkness with the light of His love for a few precious hours, and I was hungry for more. I felt like I was living out a *Raiders of the Lost Ark* script that Jesus was writing just for me. Now I'm more convinced than ever that if you want your faith to grow, you've got to be bold enough to step out. Take every opportunity He's given you and help ease someone else's pain.

But you're human, and the temptation will always be to live for yourself or to buy into the excuse that you're not good enough for God to use you. Meanwhile, your faith becomes flabby, while those few bold believers on the front lines burn out for lack of support and reinforcements.

The good news is that God still believes in you, and you can make a difference in your world. Here are some ideas for how you can join me where the action is.

Live the Life

Commit yourself to being available to God. "Here am I. Send me!" (Isa. 6:8).

The church will experience a radical transformation when we begin to concentrate on meeting the needs of the lonely people dying within the shadows of its steeples. There's no time or energy left for infighting and division when you get busy loving others to Christ and helping them grow in Him. Many Christians I meet honestly don't believe they're strong enough in their faith for God to use them in any significant way. I have news for them and you, too, if you're having a hard time picturing yourself being used by God.

To serve God, you don't have to wait until you think you're spiritually strong enough. If that were the case, I can tell you exactly how many hungry people like Gavi would get fed by believers, how many suicides would be prevented through Christian counseling, how many non-Christians would find out about Jesus' love for them, and how many Bible studies would be taught: *zero.*

Instead, you become strong because you're serving. You're out in the mix using the gifts He's given you (acting, teaching, singing, drawing, coaching, counseling, or whatever) to touch people for Him. You're in a battle for the lives of your friends, and the stakes are high enough to keep your attention. You'll find a new and healthy urgency to read your Bible because you're looking for answers that will help the people you love. Your prayer time will take on a whole new depth because you're praying for real people with real problems that you care about.

I went through a period last year when I realized I was sometimes too timid about sharing my faith verbally. You know the excuses: "I don't want to offend anyone, Lord" or

"That guy's just too tough. He'd never be interested." Well, when I finally couldn't put off the Holy Spirit's conviction any longer, I surrendered. When I told the Lord I wanted to be more available to Him, I discovered an interesting thing about the way He works. When He knows that you care more about others than about your own comfort zone, He brings all kinds of people your way and makes sharing His love with them as natural as possible.

> **The burden on you is not to be adequate; it's to be available.**

So don't worry about whether you feel adequate for the job God chooses for you. The burden on you is not to be adequate; it's to be available. Paul said, "That is why, for Christ's sake, I delight in weaknesses, in insults, in hardships, in persecutions, in difficulties. For when I am weak, then I am strong" (2 Cor. 12:10).

Believe you can make a difference. "Each one should use whatever gift he has received to serve others" (1 Pet. 4:10).

A recent survey of youth between ages thirteen and nineteen shows that the number one reason teenagers leave the church is because no one there takes them seriously enough to give them anything meaningful to do. It's a fact that people who aren't a part of the action at church either leave it, often never to return, or just put in their time, waiting for the chance to be with friends who make them feel important.

It doesn't have to be that way. You are valuable to God. He has uniquely gifted you for some kind of service, and you'll never find out what those gifts are until you run the risk of making yourself available to Him. But first you've got to believe that you can make a difference. I heard a story that might help.

One day an old man was walking the beach at dawn when he noticed a young guy ahead of him picking up starfish and flinging them into the sea. He finally caught up with the boy and asked him why he was doing this. The answer was that the stranded starfish would die if left until the morning sun came up.

"But you're wasting your time," said the old man. "This beach goes on for miles, and there are millions of starfish." Then he asked the youth, "How can your effort make any difference?"

The boy looked at the starfish in his hand, smiled softly, and then threw it to safety in the waves. "It makes a difference to this one," he said.

You are not wasting time when you do anything for God. If you make a difference for eternity in the life of just one of your friends, you have passed along a gift that is absolutely priceless.

Begin by being there for someone else. "Whatever you did for one of the least of these brothers of mine, you did for me" (Matt. 25:40).

"I'm getting desperate for someone to talk to," wrote twenty-four-year-old Sandi from Vermont,

. . . I mean really talk to about the things that are bothering me. I have a longing to be completely honest and open with someone, to let them see inside me to who I really am. But I'm so alone with my feelings. I think that just talking to someone about it would help—even if they didn't have all the answers. I've prayed and prayed for someone to talk to, but so far I've found no one. That's why I'm writing this letter. I need someone to tell me I'm not totally insane and that they love me for who I am.

Sandi's letter is not unusual. People write from all over the world with the same problem. They can't find anyone who cares. There is someone waiting for you to be there, someone who will listen to you, and possibly only to you—because you care.

I'm thinking of that person when I sing "I Will Be Here for You." Who are you thinking of?

> *I will be here for you*
> *Somewhere in the night*
> *Somewhere in the night.*
> *I'll shine a light for you*
> *Somewhere in the night.*
> *I'll be standing by*
> *I will be here for you.*[1]

Don't be afraid of trying something new for God. "Call to me and I will answer you and tell you great and unsearchable things you do not know" (Jer. 33:3).

Life is like a ten-speed bike. Most of us have gears we never use. Something happened to me at Christmastime that brought this truth home. I got the message on Christmas Day that Grandma Bocook died earlier that morning. She wasn't my real grandmother, but she was that one adult outside my home I could go to anytime about anything—especially during my rebellious years.

When I heard the news, I was shaken. I slipped into the shower to get alone with my thoughts. And somewhere between the shampoo and the creme rinse, God clearly spoke to me. I know the thought came from Him because I'd never have had it by myself.

"You need to go back to West Virginia and speak at her funeral."

It was a commission I wasn't about to accept without a fight. "There's no way I can do it, Lord. I'm not a speaker," I said out loud in the shower. "Besides, it's Christmas, and our relatives are visiting. I can't leave my family during the holidays." Then, knowing I had to do something, I decided to make a safe deal with God.

"All right, Lord. Here's what I'll do. If the Bocook family calls and asks me to preach the funeral, I'll go." Of course, I knew they wouldn't call because I'm not a preacher. I was 100 percent sure they'd find a pastor and he'd do the speaking. I was 100 percent wrong. When the call came through, I just sat at the phone shaking my head in wonder, telling them that of course I would come.

With my Bible and notes spread out before me on the plane trip back to my hometown, I put some thoughts together for a sermon. It was obvious that God had arranged for me to go, and yet, I wouldn't be honest if I told you I wasn't a little nervous about speaking. As the service began, I sang some praise songs first, and we worshiped Him for a while. Then I started preaching. At Grandma Bocook's funeral, I learned again that God will never call you to do something for Him without providing the means for you to do it.

"Do not worry about what to say or how to say it," Jesus told His disciples. "For it will not be you speaking, but the Spirit of your Father speaking through you" (Matt. 10:19, 20). God's Spirit was on me that day and I knew it. It didn't seem like I was doing something I'd never done before; it felt as if I'd been preaching all my life. And that's the way it will be for you too. You will never be more satisfied or at peace with yourself than the moment you realize that what you're doing with your life, and what He wants you to do with it, are the same.

Only one life,
Soon will be passed.
Only what's done
For Christ will last.

7.

Run to
The Battle

7
Run to the Battle
Dealing with the Devil

"There is no neutral ground in the universe. Every inch, every split second, is claimed by God and counter-claimed by Satan."
—C. S. Lewis

The hair stood up on the back of my neck and my mouth went dry. A perceptible evil brooded in the heavy night air that surrounded us. I'd faced fear on rare occasions in my life, but this was the first time I was afraid of something I couldn't see.

All I knew for sure is that Guido and I were not alone on the bridge we were inching our way across. Whatever was out there with us, we felt its hatred as surely as if it were cursing us out loud. I was so certain of its demonic presence that I was about to challenge it to come out of the shadows and show itself. Then I heard Guido's voice coming from somewhere to my left. "Smitty, we need to get out of here."

Maybe it hadn't been a good idea to leave the ballpark and try to find our hotel. In the aftermath of the largest earthquake to rock San Francisco in sixty years, I just wanted to find a place that was relatively safe. No one knew when the next shockwaves would hit, and some people were getting panicky. It didn't help matters that the quake had plunged most of the city into pitch blackness, an open invitation to looters and other dangerous types to roam the streets.

It was so dark that I remembered Jesus once saying, "Light has come into the world, but men loved darkness instead of light because their deeds were evil" (John 3:19). To this day, I don't believe there were any other humans on that bridge with us. But something inhuman with evil intent was there; something that felt more comfortable in the darkness than we did.

"Though I walk through the valley of the shadow of death," I whispered, "I will fear no evil, for you are with me" (Ps. 23:4). My voice sounded thin and powerless. With lunacy ruling the night in that corner of California, the forces against us weren't about to give up without a struggle. Just then Guido began to hum the tune of the Rich Mullins song, "Awesome God." A moment later I joined in with him. Whatever lurked about us was losing its grip and its power to intimidate.

Soon we were both singing at the top of our lungs, and the blackness we'd been shrouded in seemed a shade or two lighter.

> Our God is an awesome God
> He reigns from heaven above
> With wisdom, power, and love
> Our God is an awesome God.[1]

We approached the crest of the bridge with confidence and knew the darkness was breaking up. By the time we reached the other side, we were bathed in a light more brilliant than mere emergency generators could produce. Jesus' words came back to me. "Whoever lives by the truth comes into the light" (John 3:21).

We had passed through the middle of a battle being fought in the unseen world, and we had survived.

That experience reminded me that there is a whole other world just as real as the one I can see and smell and touch. It's the world of angels and evil spirits, of God and Satan, of heaven and hell. It's a world I often forget about in my daily rush to pay bills, run errands, and raise a family. But the cost of ignoring its reality is too high to consider. Families have been destroyed, reputations shattered, and lives tragically taken prematurely—all because people pretend that this other world doesn't exist.

Angels Unaware

Long before the Oscar-winning movie *Chariots of Fire* was filmed, a remarkable man who lived in the hills of northern Israel saw the real thing. His name was Elisha, and his best friend, Gehazi, was a lot like I am. The two of them were sleeping soundly in the early morning hours when something woke Gehazi. He stumbled outside and to his terror saw that he and Elisha were surrounded by an entire army of enemy soldiers sent to capture them. Paralyzed with fear, he raced back into the house to report the bad news to Elisha.

The prophet calmly replied, "Don't be afraid." Then he looked out the window and did a quick head count himself, telling his companion, "Those who are with us are more than those who are with them" (2 Kings 6:16). Immediately Elisha prayed for Gehazi to recognize the mighty angels on his side.

"'O Lord, open his eyes so he may see.' Then the Lord opened the servant's eyes, and he looked and saw the hills full of horses and chariots of fire all around Elisha" (2 Kings 6:17).

What Elisha did for his friend, Frank Peretti did for me when he wrote *This Present Darkness*. I already believed in the world of the supernatural, but Peretti opened my eyes to the unseen forces of good and evil that affect my life every day. I'm more aware now of angels that watch over me and my family, and of evil spirits that would ruin me if they could.

What Peretti did for me, Jesus did for His disciples in the first century. When they reported back to Him for a debriefing meeting after one of their tours, they were out of breath with excitement. They told Him all they'd done, and He interpreted it for them.

Jesus said, "I saw Satan fall like lightning from heaven" (Luke 10:18). Everything the disciples had been doing for God (preaching, traveling, studying, praying, and so on) might have seemed commonplace and insignificant to those who only see one world. Jesus looked into that other world where mighty battles are being fought over the lives of men and women. There He saw that the faith and efforts of common people make a great difference in the battles' outcomes.

Nowadays when I'm working on a song, flying off on another trip, or just sharing my faith wherever I am, I'm learning to hear Jesus' encouraging words, "I saw Satan fall like lightning, Michael." I'm learning to keep the eyes of my spirit open for the enemy's encroachment against my family. I'm seeing the importance of Paul's message to the Corinthians when he wrote, "So we fix our eyes not on what is seen, but on what is unseen. For what is seen is temporary, but what is unseen is eternal" (2 Cor. 4:18).

In other words, the invisible world is the more important one, and it's time we started paying attention to it. I'm tired of seeing kids getting beaten up on by Satan, with no clue about how to fight back. Fourteen-year-old Andy wrote this disturbing letter from Atlanta:

Dear Michael,

I'm being attacked every day by the devil and I don't know what to do. I guess it all began when I got into the game, Dungeons and Dragons. Before I started playing, no one liked me. I got good at it, though, and after I became a "dungeonmaster," a lot of guys I played with thought I was cool. But last month I realized I was getting in so deep that it was beginning to really scare me. So I decided to get out, and that's when all hell broke loose. I've been having terrible nightmares, and some guys in a satanic group at school hate me and are trying to hurt me. What can I do? I listen to your music and it helps some, but I need something more.

View from the Tomb

More than my music, Andy needs Jesus. Outside of the power and authority of Jesus Christ, I could give him no hope. It's not enough to just decide that you want nothing to do with Satan anymore. If you try to turn away from the devil without turning toward Christ, you may wind up even worse off than before. Jesus explained this Himself in a frightening story.

> When an evil spirit comes out of a man, it goes through arid places seeking rest and does not find it. Then it says, "I will return to the house I left." When it arrives, it finds the house swept clean and put in order. Then it goes and takes seven other spirits more wicked than itself, and they go in and live there. And the final condition of that man is worse than the first. (Luke 11:24–26)

Jesus also stated, "He who is not with me is against me" (Matt. 12:30).

It's like Bob Dylan once sang, "You've Gotta Serve

Somebody." There are only two powers on this planet you can choose to serve. If your choice is not Jesus, you are automatically serving Satan. Even if you don't believe in the devil, to choose self over Christ is to choose the enemy.

If, on the other hand, you give your heart to Jesus, you've allied yourself with a power that is far greater than Satan's. "The one who is in you is greater than the one who is in the world" (1 John 4:4). Never was this truth clearer than when Jesus was taken down off the cross and laid in the grave.

Soon after the stone was rolled across the entrance to the tomb, the Bible says that Jesus left his mutilated body to take an extraordinary trip. Just a few hours earlier, Satan and all the demon hordes in the cosmos were celebrating what looked like their final victory. The Lamb of God was slain. The earth was theirs to do with whatever they wished. But there was a little miscalculation in their strategy called the Resurrection, and Jesus reminded them of it during His three days and nights in the tomb. Peter recorded His incredible journey.

"He was put to death in the body but made alive by the Spirit, through whom also he went and preached to the spirits in prison who disobeyed long ago . . ." (1 Pet. 3:18–20).

The good news is that the same victory He won over Satan is yours for the asking. "I have given you authority to . . . overcome all the power of the enemy," He promised (Luke 10:19). No believer has to live outside His protection. And if you listen carefully the next time you rise from your knees after prayer, or get back in your car after visiting a nursing home, or mail a letter of hope to someone who has none, you just might hear Jesus saying, "I saw Satan fall like lightning!"

In the meantime, if you're still trying to figure out your role in the battle between heaven and hell, here's some practical advice to help you be bolder.

Live the Life

Decide whose side you're on. "No one can serve two masters" (Matt. 6:24).

I know from experience that the loneliest place in the world to be is between two kingdoms. In my first book, *Old Enough to Know*, I told the story of how I did my best to run from God's love. I was in pretty pathetic shape and knew that I either had to come back to my childhood faith or destroy what little future I had left.

> I know from experience that the loneliest place in the world to be is between two kingdoms.

Jesus said, "He who is not with me is against me" (Matt. 12:30) because He knew you can't play both ends against the middle. You'll exhaust yourself trying to figure out ways to live with your guilty conscience. It's impossible to serve two masters, and the time will come when you'll have to decide which one to follow, just like eighteen-year-old Casey, who wrote,

> My biggest problem is that I don't want to give up either side. I want it both ways; to have the best of both worlds. I want to be able to drink and try drugs and do anything else my friends are doing. But I know that's just living for the moment and when it's all over I feel cheap, and empty, and used. I want something that's real and permanent. I don't want to leave my friends, but sometimes when I'm around Christians, I wonder what I might be missing on the other side.

My advice to Casey was, "You don't have to leave your friends if you bring them with you to the other side. But if they won't come, then maybe they need to see someone who has the courage to break away." I had to make the same

decision myself, and later I looked back on it in the song
"On the Other Side":

> *I'm not how I used to be*
> *When we hung around*
> *Back when it was you and me*
> *Tearin' up this town.*
> *We used to live our lives running from change.*
> *Now we don't see eye to eye.*
> *I am not the same.*
>
> *And you wonder where I've gone.*
> *Well, I've found where I belong.*
> *I'm on the other side.*
> *True—I used to walk your shore*
> *But I'm not there anymore.*
> *I'm on the other side.*
>
> *Why is it hard for you to see*
> *All the changes made in me*
> *Here on the other side?*
> *Oh, I could help you understand*
> *And you could join me where I am.*
> *I am on the other side.*[2]

Just like Casey, eventually you'll have to give up your
double life or lose your sanity trying to live in two worlds at
once. Such a place doesn't exist. There is no neutral ground
in the universe. You will serve either God or Satan. And if
you realized how much God loves you and how much Satan
despises you, only one choice makes any sense.

Commit to live with Christ as your Lord. "Anyone who
chooses to be a friend of the world becomes an enemy of God.
Resist the devil, and he will flee from you" (James 4:4, 7).

Most people want to be delivered from temptation, but

they'd like to stay in touch with it. The Lord knows that a lukewarm faith is worse than having none at all. When it comes to Satan, God wants me to take no prisoners. I'm sure that if I eased off of my convictions and let up on my witness, I could get the enemy off my back. He would leave me alone if I just learned to leave him alone. All I'd have to do is lighten up some on my faith and be a little less radical for God. There's nothing Satan would rather do than make a friend of me. And the whole thing could happen so slowly, so subtly, that I would hardly notice that my love for God was cooling off.

> There is no neutral ground in the universe. You will serve either God or Satan.

God tells us to "hate evil and love the good" (Amos 5:15 TLB). I worry about people who can't get angry about evil. They're usually the same ones who can't get excited about goodness and righteousness either. In "Cross of Gold," I ask an important question:

> *Where do you stand? What is your statement?*
> *What is it you're trying to say?*
> *What's in your hand; what's in your basement?*
> *What's in the cards you don't play?*
>
> *Are you holding the key*
> *Or are you intending to pick*
> *the lock of heaven's gate?*
> *It's confusing to me the message you're sending,*
> *and I don't know if I can relate.*
>
> *What's your line?*
> *Tell me why you wear your cross of gold.*

State of mind? Or does it find
A way into your soul?
Is it a flame; is it a passion?
Is it a game; religion in fashion?[3]

There is a great battle being fought in the unseen world for our minds and, ultimately, our souls. God is waiting for someone to get passionate enough to get radical for Him.

Recognize who your only enemy is. "For our struggle is not against flesh and blood, but against the rulers, against the authorities, against the powers of this dark world and against spiritual forces of evil . . ." (Eph. 6:12).

I'm a competitive person. Just ask the guys I play softball, tennis, or even ping pong with. There's nothing wrong with giving your all to win, but I don't consider my athletic opponent my enemy.

In fact, I refuse to name any fellow human an enemy of mine. The moment you hate others, you give them power over you—over your sleep, your appetite, and your happiness. Even if another was completely wrong and hurt you deeply, hating that person will only hurt you.

And yet, there is within me a God-given capacity to be a fighter, to dig in my heels and turn my anger on the only adversary God will ever allow me to call my enemy. His name is Satan, and his one goal for eternity is your destruction. "Your enemy the devil prowls around like a roaring lion looking for someone to devour" (1 Pet. 5:8).

Turn your prayer weapons against the enemy. "One cannot rob Satan's kingdom without first binding Satan. Only then can his demons be cast out!" (Matt. 12:29 TLB).

In C. S. Lewis's *Screwtape Letters*, one of the chief evil spirits wrote to Wormwood, a lesser demon, these revealing words: "Interfere when people start to pray . . . real prayer is lethal to our cause." The apostle Paul knew what prayer could do to Satan when he said, "The weapons we fight with are not the weapons of the world. On the contrary, they have divine power to demolish [the devil's] strongholds" (2 Cor. 10:4).

Satan has declared open war on young people, especially in America, through music, television, movies, literature, and the spread of satanism. I can do no less than declare war on him. It's time to be bold. Through the powerful weapon of prayer, I can sabotage Satan's plans. I've come to learn that one of the real purposes of prayer isn't to persuade or influence God, but to join with Him against the enemy.

Jesus' own life and ministry will remain an unsolved riddle to you if you don't understand how much He focused His power against the devil. If you can read through the Gospels and not be struck by the importance of His prayer warfare against the powers of darkness, then you're missing a key element for your own growth. So welcome to "the other side." We've been waiting for reinforcements.

8.

When Bad Things Happen to Good People

8
When Bad Things Happen to Good People
Growing through Crises

"There will come a time when you believe everything is finished. That will be the beginning."
— Joe Bayly

Circumstances can sometimes ruin your best intentions. Such was the case that caused Debbie and me to arrive late for a good friend's funeral. We climbed the steps to the balcony and slipped quietly into two of the only seats left in the crowded church. Friends and relatives were taking turns sharing their memories of the deceased.

As Deb's grandfather, A. V. Washburn, stepped up to the microphone, she leaned forward in our pew and sighed heavily with a sadness that matched the dull ache in my own heart. The sweet old gentleman cleared his throat and spoke in a strong voice that defied his eighty-four years.

"Susan was the most compassionate person I ever met," said Grandpa Washburn. "That's probably why she made such a great nurse. I learned this firsthand because my father-in-law, whom we called Da, lived to be 100 years old and Susan had a special love for him. Of course, she made everyone who met her feel that way. Well, Da made it clear that he didn't want to die in a hospital around people who didn't know him. It was his wish to die at home where he could spend his last moments with his family. Susan made that possible.

"Whenever Da needed her, she'd drop whatever she was doing and rush to his side. When his pain was too great to endure, she would give him medication to ease his suffering. And of course, she called the moment she heard he died.

"Frequently she would say, 'Mr. Washburn, I want to come over and help you guys in any way I can.'

"That's all right, Susan, I would tell her. You've already done more than anyone could ask. You don't have to come.

"'I know that, sir,' she would reply. 'I want to come.' And so she sat with my father-in-law's body right up to the moment the ambulance arrived. It was just like Susan to love someone even beyond death."

Grandpa Washburn paused for a moment, and then he said, "And now she's gone too."

His face flushed with emotion as he closed his eulogy with, "All I can say is, heaven is a brighter place today because Susan Frierson is a full-time resident now."

I looked over at Debbie and tears filled her eyes. She and Susan had been close since they were about six years old. They were like sisters, and now she dearly missed her beloved friend. I took my wife's hand and squeezed it gently.

As one person after another rose to pay tribute to Susan, my own memories passed before me. I couldn't count the number of times Susan had been in our home, helping in any way she could. Like the night Whitney was crying because of a bad earache, and Susan showed up at the door with her odoscope to check for infection and to soothe our daughter's pain. Or the time Ryan drank some hydrogen per-oxide, and Susan called Poison Control and then spent the night nursing him back to health.

I sat in the balcony looking down at her closed casket. Ironically, it wasn't far from the spot where she stood as one of Deb's bridesmaids at our wedding ten years earlier in this same church. I felt like my heart was going to break.

A different voice was coming up from the main floor, and I recognized it as belonging to one of the nurses at the hospital where we had our fourth child, Anna. I tried to focus in on her words:

"When I first went to Westside Hospital," she said, "I was fresh out of nursing school. Please believe me when I tell you, I was absolutely lost. I didn't know what I was going to do. God must have heard my prayers, because He sent Susan into my life. Her godly witness was a constant inspiration to me. She was always smiling and always kind. Everyone loved her. She had the hands and the heart of a healer. Susan was so selfless, she was just like an angel."

Could Susan have been an angel? I wondered. *No, angels don't die in car accidents. Angels don't suffer such extensive brain damage that life-support systems are useless. And angels don't have grieving parents shattered by sorrow sitting in the front pew at their funerals. Susan was not an angel; only the death of a human could cause so many so much pain. How we miss her already, Lord.*

My reflections were temporarily broken when the officiating pastor called out my name: "And now, Michael W. Smith, a good friend of the family, will remember Susan with a song."

It takes time to work out the death of a close friend. Usually the few days before a funeral are not nearly enough. Walking to the piano, I still had some unanswered questions for God. But nonetheless, I sat down at the keyboard and began to sing. "Packing up the dreams God planted. . . ."

View from the Hearse

In *The Last Thing We Talk About*, Joe Bayly tells an incredible story of the loss of three sons: one at eighteen days, after surgery; the second at five years, from leukemia; the last one at eighteen years, after a sledding accident. I still marvel at the faith that could have him write,

> Reason, we believe, is a deceptively weak crutch for faith. Reason gropes in the dark for answers, while faith waits for God. . . . But we believe that God is love. I cannot explain it, but my wife and I have never been more convinced of His love for us and our children than when we have turned from a fresh grave.

Bayly's courage notwithstanding, it's still one thing to hear about how others deal with their tragedies and something else for you to face tragedy yourself. When it happens at your own address, you have a totally unique understanding.

Debbie and I really struggled with Susan's death. Along with many others, we'd been praying for a miraculous healing. We knew it would be a great witness to the doctors and anyone else who knew that Susan was a Christian if they saw God pull her through this crisis.

"Nothing is too hard for you, Lord," we prayed. "You could reach down and heal our friend and return her to us right now." We had great hope. Less than three days after we'd started our prayer vigil, Susan died.

The question "Why?" lingers on for us. Tragedies like this never make much sense. But no matter how much we miss her and are disappointed that God didn't choose to answer our prayers the way we wanted, we have an underlying peace that He's in control. Even at the funeral, many of us sensed that there was a Higher Reason at work behind the scenes. Without a doubt, we felt the grip of the "Hand of Providence" among us.

> The Hand of Providence
> Has been our best defense
> Though His ways are sometimes hard to understand
> From the dying of a heartbeat to another soul reborn
> From in between and circling our thoughts of love and war
> Oh, the Hand of Providence
> Is guiding us through choices that we make.[1]

If there's one thing we all have in common, it's that we have lost, or someday will lose, someone who is very important to us. When that time comes, you might be tempted to shake your fist at God and accuse Him of being either too weak or too uncaring to save the life of your friend. But there are a few things we should recognize about God when this happens.

First and foremost, God is a deeply compassionate Father. He cares about us when we suffer. He understands our anger and our confusion. His grief is just as real as ours. The Bible says, "Precious in the sight of the Lord is the death of his saints" (Ps. 116:15).

More important than God's ability to understand our pain, however, is *why* He understands it. No one knows more about the death of a loved one than He does. Never forget that He had a pretty good "view from the hearse" Himself. Could He have stopped the Romans from crucifying His Son? Of course He could have—just as easily as He could have kept Susan's little blue Toyota from hitting a telephone pole. He had His reasons for remaining silent both times. The first I understand—His Son was born to die so that I can live forever. The second I don't understand—at least not yet.

"Now we see through a glass, darkly; but then face to face: now I know in part; but then shall I know even as I am known" (1 Cor. 13:12 KJV).

I get many letters from people who are trying to put the pieces back together and wondering where God is in the mix. One sixteen-year-old girl named Mary touched my heart with her piercing questions.

Dear Michael,

If God confuses me because He seems so distant, then who can I go to when I need answers so badly? My best friend took his life last year after I begged God to save him. Now life is not worth living without him. I'm running out of resources. I can't fight much longer—don't know if I even want to. You say I'd be throwing away a lifetime, but what kind of life is it, anyway?

All I've ever wanted was somebody to be there by my side, to hold me when I hurt, to laugh with me, to do things together. The real question remains: If I can't go to God, then who can I go to? It just seems I'm not worth it anymore.

Love always,
Mary

Satan is such a liar. He torpedoes us with thoughts that God is distant and unconcerned about our suffering. Actually, the opposite is the truth. King David said, "The Lord is close to the brokenhearted and saves those who are crushed in spirit" (Ps. 34:18). You'll always find Jesus in the valley of the shadow of death, waiting for anyone who's honest enough to admit they need Him.

Sometimes I wonder how people can live without knowing God in a personal way. He's the only stable point in a world racing toward its own destruction. Too many things make no sense unless there's some kind of purpose behind all the madness, some good reason to go on living.

I wrote Mary back and told her that God had never left her. He was just waiting for her to look inside her heart and realize she couldn't make it without Him. The enemy had tried to convince her that she was no good. "On the contrary," I reminded her, "you are worth the death of God's own Son."

Live the Life

If you plan on living here in this world, then you'd better figure out how you're going to deal with crises. Suffering is unavoidable for the human race; it touches us all. Jesus warned his disciples with these words: "I have told you these things, so that in me you may have peace. In this world you will have trouble. But take heart! I have overcome the world" (John 16:33).

When it comes to hard times, you can count on your share. How you handle them when they come will probably determine who you become. Here's some advice that might help.

Consider that what you're going through might be a part of God's plan for you to grow. "Consider it pure joy . . . whenever you face trials of many kinds, because you know that the testing of your faith develops perseverance. Perseverance must finish its work so that you may be mature and complete" (James 1:2–4).

I took my son Ryan out one afternoon to teach him how to fly a kite, and I noticed something important. Kites rise against the wind, not with it. A certain amount of opposition is good for you.

I don't divide people into the weak and the strong or the successes and the failures. I divide them into people who learn from life and those who don't. When learners do something wrong, they suffer the consequences and don't do it again. And when they do something right, they do it even better the next time, without getting proud or self-righteous. Even if they suffer in some way, they tune in to hear what God is saying to them in the midst of the pain. Often I've discovered that those who have suffered the most in life become people of great character and depth.

The mountaintop, with all of its rewards, might be exciting to reach now and then. But you can't live there, though some people sure try. The reality is this: nothing grows on the mountaintop. The air is too thin and the soil too rocky. God knows that what you need for growth is the rich, black soil of the valley, and He says as much in Romans 5: "We also rejoice in our sufferings, because we know that suffering produces perseverance; perseverance, character; and character, hope" (vv. 3, 4).

In fact, I'll go even further and say that my kite rises highest when the wind against it is strongest. I'm gradually learning not to run from my problems but, instead, to thank God for them — even though the phone never stops ringing; even though I can't get my car out of the mechanic's garage; and even though I'll never see Susan's face again this side of heaven.

Looking back on my life to this point, it's the valleys that have made the greatest impact in my life, not the mountaintops. It seems that it has always been during the low points that my faith has grown. It was in the valleys that God taught me never to search for happiness but, instead, to receive His joy. It was there I learned the value of contentment and the meaning of true friendship.

When you're broken, God has His best chance to work. "The heart of the wise is in the house of mourning, but the heart of fools is in the house of pleasure" (Eccles. 7:4).

"God whispers to us in our pleasures," wrote C. S. Lewis in *The Problem of Pain*, "but He shouts in our pain. Pain is God's megaphone to rouse a deaf world." It seems that about the only time He has our complete attention is when we're in some kind of trouble.

I have a friend who reminds me that God wants just three things from us: bent knees, broken hearts, and wet eyes. And if He gets them, He can work wonders in our lives. It's not that God is trying to spoil our fun; it's just that He knows we're most available to Him when our pride is out of the way. The broken ground is most receptive to the seed.

Don't lose hope when you're going through the valley. "Though he slay me, yet will I hope in him" (Job 13:15).

Now and then I'll meet people who have no hope because they're suffering for having made bad choices. One girl wrote and insisted that she could never be a Christian since God couldn't possibly forgive her for the terrible thing she had done. Pregnant at sixteen, she was too young to get married, and her boyfriend had talked her into getting an abortion. One year later and riddled with guilt, she told me she was at the end of her rope.

Becky Pippert tells of a similar story and how she handled it. A young woman, haunted by her conscience, cried out to Becky, "I can't believe I murdered an innocent baby!"

After hearing the confession, Becky asked God for wisdom to answer the girl, and when it came, she swallowed hard and thought, "Lord, are you sure you want me to say this?" Turning toward the girl who was grieving for a child she would never know, she spoke as gently as she could. "I don't know why you're so surprised. This isn't your first murder; it's your second."

Most people will react to her statement as I did: "How could you say that to this miserable girl? That would just make her feel worse." But then, Becky explained that each of us, by being born with a natural bent toward sin, is responsible for nailing Jesus Christ to the tree.

"So you're right," said Becky. "You are worse than you thought. But the good news is, *you're forgiven!*" The cross shows me the worst thing I've ever done, and at the same time, it shows me the healing that Christ has given. *I am forgiven!*

So take courage. If you are suffering the consequences of a choice you made in the past, there is still hope and a future for you. If you want to change directions and will accept His forgiveness, nothing can separate you from His love. The time may have come, even now, when you believe everything is finished. That could be just the beginning—if you look to Jesus.

You can glorify God in your response to suffering. "If you suffer as a Christian, do not be ashamed, but praise God that you bear that name" (1 Pet. 4:16).

I read once that a famous Roman senator went to the Coliseum as a spectator during Nero's persecution of the Christians. He had joined in similar gruesome festivities before, but this was his first contact with the new religious sect, and he was curious about how these people would face death.

Not far from where he was seated, a ferocious lion stalked a young Christian girl, and the wealthy Roman was spellbound as he prepared to watch the slaughter. Just a few yards away from him, the girl bravely faced the beast in grim silence.

The senator later wrote in his journal that just as the girl was about to die before his eyes, she did something that changed his life forever. She smiled at him. The Roman was haunted by that smile for days afterward, until he could no longer run from "the God who teaches men how to die." It is said that he faced the lions himself soon after he publicly trusted in Jesus.

There's no better witness to the watching world than believers who stand firm under suffering. "Be joyful always; pray continually; give thanks in all circumstances," said Paul, "for this is God's will for you in Christ Jesus" (1 Thess. 5:16–18).

If I hadn't already been a Christian, I probably would have become one after watching Susan's parents at her funeral. Their courage was admirable; their brokenness was understandable; but their peace was impossible—unless there is a God who gives men a reason to live and grace when they die.

> There's no better witness to the watching world than believers who stand firm under suffering.

9.

Take This Gift; It Is All I Have to Give

9
Take This Gift; It Is All I Have to Give

Singing Straight to the Heart

"Music is love in search of a voice."
—Leo Tolstoy

I could never teach anyone to write music like I do—maybe because nobody ever taught me. The more I wrote through the years, the better I got at it, but the melodies have just always been there—jump-starting my brain in the morning and lingering in my mind at night. I started writing songs when I was five years old, so it's hard to remember a time when music wasn't a big part of my life. In fact, it's difficult for me to separate the impulse to create music from my passion for life.

I think I was born to make music. When I sit down to the piano, it just feels right. I'm doing what God has called me to do. Even when I was drifting from Christ during my late teens, I knew that music was going to be my life. Soon after a pathetic semester of college, I decided to make the big move to Nashville to pursue my dream of becoming a songwriter.

I'll never forget how my mom stood on the

porch and cried while I packed my few worldly possessions into a beat-up Chevy in the driveway. As I started to pull out, I saw her run back into the house and knew that she couldn't stand to watch me leave. What a sight I was! Limping out of town in a junker with a mattress stuffed into the back seat. Anyone I passed must have thought, "No way that kid's going to make it past the city limits!" But by the time I got to the freeway, I knew I was never going back. I felt it in my bones. Even though I wasn't thinking much about God at the time, deep down inside I knew that music was His call on my life.

And let the record show: My heart is in Christian music. That's where I came from, and I know I'll never leave it. It wouldn't be me to record an album of love songs and not focus on my relationship with Christ. At the same time, I don't set out to make a "Christian album" when I walk into the studio. Instead, I purpose to create something that is true to who and where I am at that time. Because my faith is the most important thing in my life, the songs are naturally going to draw people closer to God.

How many times have I been asked, "Is 'Place in This World' a pop song or a Christian song?" It's a tough question to answer because it's the wrong one to ask. The real question should be, "Am I being true to what God is doing in my life and does my music reflect that kind of honesty?" The problem with categorizing songs is that you can begin fabricating music for a certain market, and before you know it, you're duping yourself and living a lie.

That's why I loved the *I'll Lead You Home* project. I wasn't afraid to express my failures and show the listeners my inner struggles. I think it's the purest and most honest thing I've ever done. God tapped a well inside me that I didn't even know was there.

View from My Heart: The Leesha Story

When my heart spills over because God has intersected my life with someone else's, the runoff usually grows into a new song. It could be another's great joy that touches me, and so a song like "Great Is the Lord" is born. Or it could be a heart-breaking tale that inspires a song like "I Hear Leesha." Whatever the source, the story must be one that can best be told through music. "A tragedy is a thing that will not go into words; it feels like music," wrote Mark Twain. Only music could have truly told a story like Leesha's.

The song began in my heart on the first Sunday after New Year's. A friend at church stood up and reported that two sisters, both teenagers, had been involved in a terrible accident not far from my house just the day before. As he related the tragic details, I was deeply moved in my spirit. More than once I had to catch my breath as I listened to the story.

"Leesha and Heather borrowed their dad's pickup truck to go to the store yesterday," he said, "but they never got there. They were driving along Berry's Chapel Road when a dog ran out in front of them. Heather swerved to miss the dog, but the truck crashed into a tree.

"Heather suffered a shattered nose and leg, but Leesha wasn't wearing her seat belt, so she went through the windshield. Both girls were rushed to Vanderbilt Hospital where Heather made it through the night. Leesha was not that fortunate."

I sat in my pew stunned, feeling as if I'd lost my own daughter. This was not a tragedy I would be able to pass off easily just because it happened to someone else. I felt an immediate kinship with Leesha's family, and for the next two weeks I anonymously checked in on her surviving sister's condition. I couldn't get Heather off my mind.

When a basketball player starts hitting every shot he takes, he explains it by saying, "I was just in a zone. I couldn't miss if I tried." He can't tell you how he got in that zone or when it might happen again. It just suddenly comes over him. I think that's exactly what God does to me when I get zoned in on someone who's hurting and needs a brother to care. Heather had my attention, and I could no more forget about her than I could later keep from writing the song she inspired.

As soon as I heard that she had gone home from the hospital, I knew that I had to call at her house. "What do I say if her mother answers the phone?" I thought. There are no easy answers when a child dies, and trusting God for them has come slowly for me. I exhaled deeply and dialed the number.

> *Lord knows why He's taken her away.*
> *It isn't very clear, no, it isn't very clear . . .*[1]

When her mom said hello, I nervously said, "My name is Michael W. Smith, and I'm calling to find out how Heather is doing."

"Oh, yes, we know who you are," she replied. "It's so nice of you to call."

She was a very gracious lady and gave me permission to come and visit Heather on more than one occasion. During one of my visits, Heather was obviously excited to tell me something.

"Michael!" she exclaimed. "I had an incredible dream last night that seemed as real to me as talking to you right now."

"What did you dream, Heather?" I asked.

"That God took me to where Leesha was," she said. "It's like He knew how much I needed to see her. We talked for a while, and Michael, she told me not to worry. She said that she was all right. Then we hugged each other, and I knew she was okay."

The tears silently began to form. "Did she say anything else to you?" I asked, trying to maintain my composure.

"Yes, she did, but only because I kept asking her the same question over and over. I wanted to know what it was like. 'Just what is heaven like, Leesha?' I asked her. And she said, 'Oh, Heather, you're going to love it! It's wonderful! It's absolutely wonderful!'"

When I left their home, I went straight to my studio with a heart that was spilling over. Sometimes I can express things with music before finding the right words to say what I'm feeling. That night, I wept softly the whole time I wrote "I Hear Leesha." The music flowed as freely as my tears, and when I was done, I felt an incredible peace.

Every animal leaves behind some trace of what he was. But God made humans alone to leave traces of what He created. Allowing me to enter into that creative process with Him is God's way of helping me resolve the really tough questions in life—like, Why do children have to die? I'm sure Heather could answer that question for you today: "Leesha's gone, but she will still survive."

> *I hear Leesha*
> *Singing in heaven tonight*
> *And in between the sadness*
> *I hear Leesha*
> *Telling me that she's all right.*

My music comes out of my life, and I know that's why some people are touched by it. Almost every night on the *Go West, Young Man* tour, I had to close my eyes when I sang about Leesha because so many people in the crowd were crying. When I looked up and saw them, I knew that I wasn't alone in having lost a loved one. My hope was—and is—that we share more than loss and sorrow; I pray we can look forward in hope to a reunion where we'll join Leesha and a multitude of others singing in heaven.

Live the Life

If I hadn't known it before we had mainstream success with "Place in This World," I certainly would have learned by now that music can be a controversial subject. It's just like the enemy to get people fighting over a gift from God as sublime as music.

Music is a topic that everyone seems to have a strong personal opinion about. Please consider the following as nothing more than that: my personal views. As long as we agree on the Lordship of Jesus Christ and obey His command to go boldly into the world with His love, then we can agree to disagree about styles of music without breaking our basic Christian unity. So for what it's worth, I offer you some thoughts about one of my favorite subjects.

Stay open to a rich variety of musical expressions. "Where the Spirit of the Lord is, there is freedom" (2 Cor. 3:17).

I think of music as a menu. Just as I can't eat the same thing every day, there's no single style of music that can satisfy my artistic need to create or my basic desire to listen. I've been influenced by everything from the Beatles to gifted orchestrators like James Horner (*An American Tail*) and John Williams (most of Spielberg's films); from rockers like Elton John to classical musicians like Handel, Mozart, and Chopin.

One reason I don't believe we should make a hard rule that says Christians must listen only to Christian music is that we'd miss out on so much good music that God could use to encourage us. For example, I've been deeply inspired by some of Don Henley's songs because they're about life's real issues. In "Heart of the Matter," Henley bares his soul to address the importance of forgiveness in relationships, and I can feel God's pleasure when I listen to it. I can't hear that tune without wanting to be more vulnerable and honest myself. And yet, most Christian radio stations wouldn't consider giving airplay to a song like that because it's not technically Christian music.

How did we get so good at separating the secular from the sacred, and what makes us think that it's God's best plan for us? It wasn't always that way in biblical times. Old Testament believers lived by the motto "Life is one," and they didn't waste time qualifying the activities of their days. To plow their fields and raise their children was no less spiritual for them than to read the Law of Moses. They were just as much in touch with God while being intimate with a spouse as they were reciting the Ten Commandments.

I agree that we should draw boundary lines between good and evil. You can't indiscriminately listen to or view just any art form that's available to you today. We live in a fallen world with few moral restraints, and we need to use as much wisdom as we've got. There are many songs and videotapes that will never gain entrance into my home because their very essence is anti-Christ. "I will set before my eyes [and ears] no vile thing," said King David (Ps. 101:3).

However, we live in a world that still bears enough of the stamp of its Creator that remnants of both God's truth and beauty are available in it for everyone to enjoy. Living among us and being moved by the same natural wonders that inspire us to worship Him are non-Christian authors, composers, and artists who occasionally mirror His image even though they've not been reached yet with the good news of Jesus' love.

Each time they sing, write, play, paint, or sculpt an aspect of God's creation, I believe He can be glorified by it—because

He doesn't separate the secular from the sacred. Subjects like vocation, family, sexuality, death, and ethics are just as important to Him as prayer, Bible study, tithing, and church attendance.

I'm at peace with where God has me in my career right now. Of course, there will be detractors who will say that I'm rejecting my Christian roots because some of my songs don't mention God by name — and they will be wrong. That same criticism was made of the Book of Esther, which doesn't name the Lord once in any of its chapters. Early on, many scholars wanted to keep it from being included in the Bible. But God's presence and Spirit energize each turn of that wonderful story, and today the book remains as one of the most inspiring in all of Scripture.

In the same way, God's love is the one thread that runs through all of my music and ties each new album to the last one. But the voice of the critic will probably not be stilled as long as God leads me into uncharted waters. And that's okay. I count no man as my enemy — especially a fellow believer. In fact, I'm glad there are people who care enough to "contend for the faith." It sure beats apathy.

I think it's important to look for God in more than one little corner of His creation. Then you'll never be lacking for surprises or wholesome entertainment. Just remember: "Life is one," and if your heart is right, you can be as close to Him when you're holding a tennis racquet as when you're holding a prayer book. I don't believe any symphony orchestra ever played music more inspiring to God than the sound of a two year-old laughing with a puppy. Enjoy the good things He has given you.

Use your music to help others. "Since God so loved us, we also ought to love one another" (1 John 4:11).

Musicians have traditionally developed a reputation for

being self-centered, short-tempered, and insensitive to people around them. I know that some of that perception stems from the incredible amount of energy and focus it takes for the artist to perfect the craft. Regrettably, some musicians ignore God's command to "do nothing out of selfish ambition or vain conceit, but in humility consider others better than yourselves" (Phil. 2:3).

Few things disturb me more than to see musicians, at local churches or on the professional stage, so full of themselves that they've forgotten their call to serve others. God doesn't give out His gifts for self-glory. Self-consumed artists may have talent, but they have no gift.

While recording a recent album with Wayne Kirkpatrick and the guys from the old band, a wave of gratitude passed over me. "Lord," I marveled, "it's hard to believe that You allow me to make a living at something I love to do so much." And even as I thought it, I knew it was more than just the music I loved; it was the sense of wonder of what God may do with it.

Never underestimate how God can use music in your life. "Speak to one another with psalms, hymns and spiritual songs" (Eph. 5:19).

Music seems to be a birthright for every human being. You can see its natural grip on little children when you catch them unaware riding their tricycles, combing their dolly's hair, or playing in the tub. They sing, or whistle, or hum simply for the joy of expressing the music God has planted inside them. Sometimes I wonder if infants wouldn't sing before they spoke if left to themselves.

If you pay attention to His music in your life, God can even use it to bring healing to yourself. The Bible says that King Saul was suffering from demonic oppression and teetered on the edge of sanity. But "whenever the Spirit from God came upon Saul, David would take his harp and play. Then relief would come to Saul; he would feel better, and the evil spirit would leave him" (1 Sam. 16:23).

Music can do more than simply entertain. It can be a vehicle for God's mighty power to work. In the Old Testament, when Israel's army marched into battle, God made sure that the musicians led the attack. On at least one occasion, the blast of their trumpets and the people's voices raised together caused the enemy to surrender.

I get many letters documenting the impact God can make through music. One young woman wrote,

Dear Michael,

This has been a terrible summer. In June I lost my job, and in July, my mother, who was my best friend, died suddenly. I went into a severe depression. Then a friend invited me to go to your concert. Filled with anger, I sat in the auditorium that night, daring you or anyone else to try to change my mind about how mad I was at God. As it turned out, you didn't have to. God changed me. As soon as you began singing, I could literally feel the layers of anger peeling away and the healing begin. Thank you so much.

In His love,
Pamela

Perhaps God wants to do some healing in your life too, and His plan could be to use music to do it. Whether you think you have any musical talent or not, I'm sure of one thing: He's put a song inside you. My advice is to let it come out.

"Sing and make music in your heart to the Lord, always giving thanks to God the Father for everything" (Eph. 5:19, 20).

10.

He's Waiting for You

10
He's Waiting for You
What Jesus Means to Me

"Many people today want God's help but not his interference. They have to learn that Jesus must first be Lord—or He can never be Savior."
—A. W. Tozer

"He was no wimp. How could any man take the physical torture He did, unless He was one of the toughest men who ever lived? He'd grown up in a rugged country and on that dark Friday morning, His lean, muscular body faced its hardest test—being nailed to the cross."

I stood quietly in the shadows of a blazing campfire and listened to my good friend Joe White, founder of Kannakuk-Kanakomo Camps, passionately deliver his famous Cross-Talk I'd heard so much about. More than two hundred streetwise, inner-city kids surrounded Joe, hanging on his every word.

"He'd already absorbed more pain than most humans could endure. Falsely arrested by His own people, He was brave enough to bear incredible abuse without crying out or saying a word. First, they tried and convicted Him illegally. Then they tied Him to a post and the whole gang of them beat His face with clubs and spit on Him.

"After a night of unspeakable horror, He was dragged off to be whipped by professional executioners. They used whips made of a board wielding nine strips of leather with a jagged piece of bone or metal attached to each strip. They flogged Him until He no longer resembled a human being, but they stopped just short of His death. His murder was to be kept for the world's most wicked instrument of death: the cross."

The street kids who listened to Joe understood his talk better than most people could. They knew all about false arrests, betrayal, murder, and abuse. In fact, their only escape from those things was this eight-day adventure at Kannakuk. And now Joe had his chance to spiritually prepare them to go back to the projects of Chicago, St. Louis, Dallas, Nashville, and other cities, to pierce the ghetto's darkness with God's love.

Few of those inner-city youth had ever seen anything like Kannakuk before. Swimming pools and waterslides, three meals a day and a staff of adults who genuinely loved them, campfires under a starry sky, and sleep uninterrupted by police sirens must have seemed a lot like heaven for most of them.

Still, the first few days of camp usually found counselors breaking up fights and patiently keeping rowdy kids in line. But by Friday night's Cross-Talk, the campers had changed. They'd learned more about God every day, and as Joe drew his message to its powerful conclusion, I sensed that many of them were about to make the most important decision of their young lives.

"After they beat Him senseless, He was forced to carry a heavy crossbeam on His back through city streets lined with curious onlookers, some bloodthirsty, some horror stricken. He staggered under His hundred-plus pound burden but finally made it to the place of His public execution, a hill called the Place of the Skull.

"They threw Him on His back and drove a nail through each wrist, viciously securing Him to the crossbeam. Then they placed His left foot over His right and with brute force pounded an eight-inch spike through both feet at once and deep into the wood. His eyes rolled and His mind threatened to explode with the pain. But He remained silent.

"It was only the strength of His will that kept Him conscious. He still had some things left to do while He hung there between heaven and hell. He still had to take everything bad about us, every crime we'd ever committed, every evil thought we'd ever had, and pay the penalty for them—with His life. The longest day of His thirty-three years was only half over."

All eyes were on Joe as he described Jesus' six hours on the cross. By the time he finished, every camper understood the high price God had paid for them. It was a love story like none they'd ever heard, and, one by one, hard hearts began to melt. He paused for a moment and gave them time to let the truth sink in. Then Joe offered them a choice.

"Because Jesus never sinned, He's the only one who could take the punishment for our sin. And now you have a decision to make. I've already made mine. The question is: Who will you serve from now on? You can choose yourself or you can choose God."

Joe explained exactly what it means to follow Christ and warned each of us to carefully count the cost before deciding.

"Let me tell you something," he said, his voice charged with conviction. "You'll never be the same again if you ask Jesus Christ into your heart. He'll start changing you little by little from the inside out. It won't be as easy to be selfish and dishonest anymore. You'll start telling the truth because the Truth is going to be living inside you. You'll start loving people you didn't even like before because when you make Him

Lord, you begin to see people the way He does. So count the cost, you guys. Becoming a believer is the miracle of a moment; you can do it right now. Being a believer takes a lifetime."

What happened next was extraordinary. It was that miraculous moment when God's awesome power and our desperate need meet with eternity in the balance. Many of the kids were weeping; some continued to look up at Joe standing by a rough-hewn cross erected earlier by the staff. Others stared into the campfire, their eyes glistening with tears. Several sat with their heads bowed, listening to another voice. I knew God was passing through the ranks, and I was privileged to be a part of it.

I feel like I have the gift of discernment. By that, I mean I can usually tell when something or someone isn't for real. I've traveled too far and seen too much to be fooled by religious hoaxes. What I saw that night was genuine; it was nothing less than God making contact with underprivileged kids who probably had never believed that He cared enough to walk their streets with them.

I watched juvenile delinquents sobbing while they scribbled on pieces of paper, every crime they'd committed or sin that had tripped them up. Then, with heartfelt repentance, one after another picked up a hammer and a nail, walked over to Joe, and crucified the incriminating list onto the cross beside him.

It was an experience I'll never forget, and it reconfirmed my belief that you can change the world with love—even the seemingly hopeless world of an inner-city kid. Later in the evening, I asked Joe if I could visit one of the fifteen boys' cabins for devotions. I sat cross-legged on a hardwood floor in the middle of a cabin illuminated only by a fading flashlight.

The room was thick with the presence of angels celebrating and the Spirit of God listening while ten young boys offered up gut-wrenching prayers, most of them for the first time ever. I was overcome with compassion for them and began to weep when I heard them pray.

"God, I don't know You so good yet," sniffled a thirteen-year-old named Robby, "but I believe in You. So I'm askin' You a big favor. It's my mom; she's doing drugs and she's messed up bad. I know there's nothin' You can't do, so help her, God. Please, help her."

I listened to tearful requests for God to help brothers in prison, sisters who were hookers, friends in gangs, and fathers who were long gone. As each kid finished his prayer, a counselor slipped his arm around that camper's shoulders to pray for him.

"He's here," I thought. "He's doing it again — just like He reached out to me so long ago."

It felt so right hanging out with those kids. They'd already experienced more suffering and pain than most people do in a lifetime. That night, they discovered that Jesus has a special love for them because He "came to seek and to save what was lost" (Luke 19:10). "Come to me, all you who are weary and burdened," He said, "and I will give you rest" (Matt. 11:28).

The carpenter from Nazareth was a man who was boldly involved in His world, and I left Kannakuk camp more determined than ever to be the same. Jesus refused to confine His love to the few who thought they deserved special treatment. He was a people-person, and helping them get out of trouble was His constant mission. He wasn't particularly concerned about their religion or their social status; He wanted their hearts.

I love what George McLeod said about Him:

Jesus wasn't crucified in a cathedral between two candles, but on a cross between two thieves, on the town garbage heap, on a crossroad so cosmopolitan that they had to write His title in Hebrew and in Latin and in Greek, or shall we say, in English, in Bantu, and in Africaans—at the kind of place where cynics talk smut, thieves curse, and soldiers gamble, because that is where He died, and that is what He died about, and that is where Christians should be and what Christians should be about. Jesus Christ died in the world, for the world. It seems to me we should be following His lead.

View from the Prophets

A few summers ago in Jerusalem, I was standing in the sunshine outside the Yad Vashem war memorial to the six million Jews who died in World War II. Even though I was wearing dark sunglasses, it was obvious that some Israeli schoolgirls had recognized me. I remember wondering how my music had reached the capital city of Israel, but the more they whispered among themselves, giggling and pointing in my direction, the more certain I was that I'd been spotted.

Sure enough, one of them broke away from her friends and timidly approached me. I noticed the pen and paper in her hand, so I greeted her warmly.

"Hi there," I said, knowing what would come next.

"C-c-could we get your autograph?" she stuttered.

"I'd love to," I replied and did my best to make it legible. Then I handed the paper back to the dark-eyed girl. Without looking at it, she turned and ran toward her waiting friends. You can imagine my surprise when I heard her squealing, "I did it! I did it! I got MacGyver's autograph!" You can imagine her surprise when she and her friends finally read the piece of paper.

Being mistaken for the TV star Richard Dean Anderson was a riot, and our tour group got a good laugh out of it. But the whole thing reminded me that the one I'd really like people to think of when they see me, or hear my songs, or meet my family, is the One who gives my life purpose in the first place.

What a kick it would be to walk into a room full of people who don't know you and have them think of Him simply because you're there. That's exactly what happened with the disciples in Acts 4. After they'd been thrown in jail, Peter and John were so filled with God's love and wisdom that their enemies were astonished by them. Knowing that the disciples were unschooled, ordinary men, they reasoned, "It must be because these men had been with Jesus." I can't think of a compliment I'd rather receive.

The incident with the Israeli schoolgirls wasn't the worst case of mistaken identity I've ever heard about. No, that happened when Jesus walked some of the same streets that I traveled almost two thousand years later.

Even in His own land, said the apostle John, and among His own people, He was not accepted. Most of His countrymen didn't seem to have a clue that Jesus was God in the flesh. And yet, to those who had eyes to see, who else could He have been? Raising people from the dead, healing the sick with a touch of His hand, claiming to be God and then proving it with the Resurrection, Jesus was clearly who He said He was. Only people who didn't want to see the truth could have missed Him. In fact, to discourage anybody from following Him, His enemies actually spread the lie that Jesus was the devil himself. Talk about mistaken identities!

If the leaders of His day had paid more attention to the words of their own prophets, I would never have had a reason to write "Secret Ambition." God's ambition to become a man and eventually die on a cross for the sins of all men was never meant to be a secret. The people had plenty of prophecies that should have pointed them directly to Jesus being God's own Son. But the sad truth was,

> *Nobody knew His secret ambition.*
> *Nobody knew His claim to fame.*[1]

There's no more dangerous group in the world than narrow-minded religious bigots who want God only on their terms. "Secret Ambition" goes on to say:

> *Old men watch from the outside*
> *Guarding their prey.*
> *Threatened by the voice of the paragon*
> *Leading their lambs away*
> *Leading them far away.*

They crucified their Messiah so they could get His voice out of their heads. Every time He said something like, "Love your enemies," or "You hypocrites! Don't judge others or you will be judged," or "Not everyone who says to me, 'Lord, Lord,' will enter the kingdom of heaven," He was signing His own death warrant. If you think about it, He didn't leave them

> It's ironic, but sometimes I think that modern religion is doing its best to keep God at a distance.

much choice. Either they heard His words and obeyed Him as Lord, or they only listened to His words and murdered Him for saying them.

It's ironic, but sometimes I think that modern religion is doing its best to keep God at a distance. While lonely, hurting people cry out for answers, we offer them rituals and rules instead of a relationship with their Creator. Do we do that because Jesus Christ is as much of a threat to us today as He was to those who crucified Him twenty centuries ago?

Religious types can live for themselves if they can keep God at a comfortable distance. But as soon as you call Him "Jesus," God is right by your side—demanding that you love others as much as yourself. Jesus is "God in your face," loving you and caring for you but also challenging you to change and to grow. This world doesn't need more religions or denominations. They've only served to separate us from each other. What we need is Jesus Christ.

It's possible that before you started this chapter, you knew something about Jesus but you never knew Him personally. Nothing would give me more joy than to introduce you to Him and have you make Him a friend forever. You've discovered the entrance ramp to the road to life. He's been waiting for you.

Live the Life

Accept the fact that God loves you for who you are. "This is love: not that we loved God, but that he loved us and sent his Son as an atoning sacrifice for our sins" (1 John 4:10).

I've learned in my travels that it's not an easy thing to really know people, mainly because they're not only themselves. They're also the region where they were born and the high-rise apartment or suburban home where they learned to walk. They're the games they played as children, the teachers they had in school, the poets they read, the food they ate, the music they enjoyed, the sports they loved, and the churches they attended. I seldom make the mistake of telling someone, "I know how you feel." The truth is that you can know them, truly and deeply, only if you are them.

God understood this too. That's why He sent His Son to be one of us. The Bible says that Jesus can sympathize with our weaknesses because He was "tempted in every way, just as we are" (Heb. 4:15). There's nothing about you He doesn't understand. He knows what it's like to feel lonely, betrayed, angry, and stressed out. He understands why you're like you are because He was just like you—a real person living in a world with real problems.

I refused to do the "Secret Ambition" video for a full year. Even though I was being encouraged to put the story of Jesus to that song, I told my managers that I was reluctant to do the video for one simple reason: I didn't want Jesus to come off looking weak and incompetent like He does in so many movies. I'd never seen Him portrayed as I'm sure He was: virile and passionate, an enthusiastic lover of people, capable of great joy as well as deep sorrow. Even after I finally agreed to do it, I still had my doubts.

To make the video more authentic, we decided to shoot my scenes out West in a location that resembles the wilderness of Judea, and later to mix those with the "Jesus scenes" that were filmed at a famous passion play in Arkansas.

I flew first to Tulsa, then boarded a little "puddle-jumper" that took me two hours deeper into the desert. Finally I drove another hundred miles into a remote area in Western Oklahoma. I probably could have made it to Israel in the same amount of time!

Returning home from the film site the next day, I had some time to think. I couldn't help wondering what the final project would look like. In particular, I wondered what Jesus would look like. Would people see that He wasn't a weak pawn in the hands of stronger men? Would the actor be another embarrassment to those of us who follow the real One? I could hardly wait to find out.

If you've seen the video, then you know I wasn't disappointed. In fact, the Christ that I saw in the "Secret Ambition" final edit literally blew me away. Here was a hero who was man enough to drive the wicked money changers out of the temple and God enough to rise from the dead; man enough to take our place on the cross and God enough to forgive us for putting Him there.

Here's the best part. The real meaning behind the amazing story of God's Son coming to earth for His rendezvous with death is that you were on His mind the whole time. He loves you that much. He's done everything necessary to give you life. What you do with that offer and the rest of your life is up to you.

Pick out someone to love today the way God loves you. "Jesus Christ laid down his life for us. And we ought to lay down our lives for our brothers" (1 John 3:16).

Often after Jesus performed some act of mercy, the Bible says He felt power go out of His body. I'm sure there were evenings when He was so wasted, He must have wondered how He could face the crowds the next morning. Still, He was always there for them when they needed Him.

Sometimes after a concert I feel like I've got nothing left to give, and my body tells me to go back to my dressing room and crash. I usually don't pay much attention to what it says because I know why I make music in the first place. Those faces in the audience have names, and stories behind the names, and needs within the stories. Even if I can only spend time with a few of them personally, I always feel better when I leave an arena if I've had the chance to do that.

You may not have much in the way of worldly wealth to help people out, but I've learned that time is a more valuable gift than money. There are people in your world who need you to spend some time loving them today. On the album *Change Your World*, you can hear them crying,

Somebody love me, come and carry me away.
Somebody need me, to be the blue in their gray.

michael w. smith

Somebody want me, the way I've always dreamed it could be.
Won't somebody love me, love me?[2]

Once you know Him, give someone else a chance to do the same. "Freely you have received, freely give" (Matt. 10:8).

After the apostle Paul saw Jesus on the road to Damascus, there wasn't much else he wanted to talk about for the rest of his life. You might find that the same thing will happen to you. Maybe the greatest thing you can ever do is to see Him and then tell others what you've seen in a plain way.

Don't worry about making what you've seen complicated. God's love is so simple that children seem to have a better grasp of it than adults. Most of us try to make it harder to understand than it is. As a musician, I know that creativity has nothing to do with making the message complex. Anybody can play weird; that's too easy. What's really hard is to be as simple as Bach or Bob Dylan. Making the simple complicated is common; but making the complicated simple, awesomely simple — like God becoming a man — that's creativity.

So keep it simple. Wait for the right opening and just tell your friends what you've seen. Then God will do the rest.

To see Jesus clearly and then share your vision with others — that's a goal worth giving your life to. I've done my best in this chapter to help you see Him. Now I'm hoping you can pass it along to someone else. It's time to be bold.

11.

I Believe in Love

11
I Believe in Love
Why I Am Who I Am

"If I were to begin life again, I should want it as it was. I would only open my eyes a little more."
—Jules Renard

It was one of the most interesting requests I ever got in a letter.

Dear Michael,

My name is Tiffany, and I'm fifteen years old. I want to get your latest album, but before I buy it, would you please do me a favor? I think it's important to know what a musician believes so you can understand his songs better. If I knew more about you as a person, I could appreciate why you write what you do. I guess what I'm asking for is a statement of your beliefs. Please send one soon. Thank you.

I've received quite a few letters through the years but never one that asked me for a statement of my beliefs. I was impressed with Tiffany's depth and touched by her sincerity. Tempted to mail her a Bible, I thought better of it—and wrote this book instead. We've come a long way together in the past ten chapters. Somehow I feel closer to you and Tiffany now than when I started writing.

I haven't held much back and I hope that you haven't minded. Maybe the next time you hear one of my songs, you'll understand it better because you understand me better. In fact, by now you've got a pretty good idea of exactly how I feel about the most important issues in life.

It's been good for me to tell you my stories. Have you ever written a letter to a friend and, even if you got no response, just felt better because you got it all out? I think that's what has happened to me in writing this book. I've been able to look back on my life and see more clearly the path I've traveled so far.

Some people have complex worldviews that seem to change with the seasons and would take a philosopher to figure out. My beliefs are simple, but they explain who I am and why I do the things I do.

I wish this last chapter could be a face-to-face meeting between us instead of an author/reader thing. I'd like to be able to look into your eyes when we finally say good-bye. I guess if I could sum up what I've written so far and at the same time help you express your own beliefs, this is what I would say:

I *believe* that a good friend is one of the greatest gifts you'll ever receive. I saw a bumper sticker on a Jaguar convertible that announced, "The one who dies with the most toys wins!" Anyone who thinks that's true is in for a rude awakening someday. Material things aren't the measure of our success; friends are.

You've met many of my friends in this book, and you know how I feel about accountability. There's no doubt about it: The best mirror is a friend's eye. If you find someone who loves you enough to tell you the truth about yourself, hold on to that person. You're going to need him or her if you expect to stand up against all the pressures that will come your way.

Sometimes a majority just means all the fools are on the same side. In fact, there have been times in my life when I knew I was headed in the right direction just because most people were going the other way. When the crowd pushes you to do something you know you shouldn't, it's easier to "just say no" if you have a friend saying it with you.

> Sometimes a majority just means all the fools are on the same side.

I believe there's nothing here on earth that's more important than family. I was fortunate to grow up with a mom, dad, and sister who really cared about me and each other. During the times when I was out of control, they always loved me and let me know that forgiveness was there for the asking. Even if your family life has been a complete disaster to this point, God can be a wonderful Father to you. He has a pretty good track record for helping people start over again.

The best advice I could give you about your family is to learn to enjoy the little things that can make your home a good place to be: a hug to start the day, an encouraging note slid under a bedroom door, warm laughter around the supper table, intimate talks and family prayers at bedtime. If your homelife is difficult, maybe you can simply be grateful for a day without arguments or little glimmers of hope that let you know that God can turn things for the better.

The fact is that most of us are going to miss out on life's most prestigious honors. But we're all eligible for the small pleasures that make life worthwhile. Enjoy whatever time you have left with your family.

I believe that all the answers you need for the most important questions in life are in a book called the Bible. When you're out of touch with yourself, you're out of touch with everyone else. Reading the Word keeps me in touch with myself. It's the only book I know with a life of its own, and I am most alive when it's working inside me.

Few things have had more of an impact on my life than the time I've spent in the Bible. If you're like me, you won't always agree with others' interpretations of what you find in its pages, but that's all right. It's better for you to study it for yourself anyway.

I believe that most worries are reruns and a total waste of time. Praying is always better than worrying, and it gets me in contact with a Power greater than myself. It always amazes me that, no matter how hectic my schedule is, when I break away to pray, it's as if time no longer exists. I know He's even busier than I am, yet He's never failed to meet with me. He already knows your heart, and He's just waiting for you to open it to Him. You never have to worry about saying the right thing to Him.

I come back from my times alone with God energized to start again and with a fresh reminder of why I'm working in the first place. It's enough just to be with Him and to put my problems back into perspective. So the next time you're tempted to lose sleep over something that's bothering you, do what I do: Every evening I turn my worries over to God. He's going to be up all night anyway.

I believe the Church is never going to be any stronger than the people who belong to it—and there's not one of us without weaknesses. The last time I checked, only one Man ever lived perfectly what He believed, so the rest of us should learn how to forgive and help each other when we fail.

All these years later, words still have a profound effect on people. We'd be wiser to say nothing than to criticize people who've already paid the consequences for the bad choices they've made. The Church could do more good than any other organization on earth if it would realize and live by one simple truth: If you harshly judge people, you have no room left in your heart to love them.

I believe that it is important to proactively care about all those around you. The difference between Jesus and most people is that when He asks you how you're doing, He waits to hear the answer. If you really want to find your place in this world, you'll discover that it's right next to a person who needs your help.

It might be the guy who sits behind you in class whose parents are going through a divorce, or the girl in your carpool who has no friends, or that gray-haired lady at your church who lost her husband last month. Lonely, hurting people are everywhere, so it won't be hard to find one.

Don't believe the lie that God couldn't use you to help them. It's time to be bold. The only thing you need is a loving heart and faith that God can do anything. Listen to the wise counsel of good friends but not to the cynics and scoffers. In the words of Paul, "Don't let anyone look down upon you because you are young" (1 Tim. 4:12). Don't believe those who say that you're taking too big a chance. Michelangelo would have painted the Sistine floor with that kind of faith, and it would have been rubbed out by now.

I believe that the only real enemy I'll ever have is the evil one himself. I won't fall victim to hating any man or woman; I know I'm as human and fallible as the next guy. I know who's behind much of the suffering in the world anyway. So I save my anger for the demonic mind that delights in seeing babies die, children starve, soldiers kill, and families break up.

One of the best things that could happen to you is to realize that you have an alert and very personal enemy whose sole purpose is to bring you down. He's been a liar from the beginning, and his latest trick is to get you to ignore him. He's more likely to leave you alone if you will leave him alone. You'd be wiser and stronger if you didn't.

I believe that you don't grow until you hurt. The deepest people I know are the ones who have suffered the most and have not let it destroy them. I've learned that bitterness is never lonely; self-pity always tags along. When you're too busy feeling sorry for yourself, you're too nearsighted to see the lesson behind the suffering. It's impossible to mature if you complain about every setback—just like it's impossible to lose if you learn from your defeats. Sure, mountaintops are fun to climb, but valleys are where things grow best.

I believe that good music is judged not by what it sounds like, but what it does to us. Someone once said that inside every person, there's a poet who died young. That doesn't have to be true. Music is God's way of keeping the poet alive inside all of us. Its genius is that it can reach the heart when nothing else can. An honest song can wash away the dust of everyday life from your soul and give you strength to go on.

The older we get, the more we tend to get caught up in the busyness of life and the harder it is to be touched by a song. Take my advice. Stay young forever, and don't turn off the music He's put inside you.

I believe the most important decision you'll ever make is what to do about Jesus Christ. There's a good reason that ours is a world of nuclear giants and ethical infants. We know more about war than we do about peace, more about killing than about living. Why? Because we've grasped the mystery of the atom but rejected the One who created it.

I had a friend who used to say, "If you hit the ball over the fence, you can take your time going around the bases." This is what life is all about. When God sent His Son to die for me, and I trusted Him with my heart, that was the home run that allows me to contentedly enjoy going around the bases of life.

When God cared enough to send the very best, it was Jesus who taught us the true meaning of love. He was the "prophet from the Land of Wise," and His song hasn't changed for two thousand years.

> *Love one another*
> *Love one another,*
> *'Cause you know without a doubt,*
> *You can change your world with love.*

This book has been about the people that I have come to love: Ashley, Bryn, Leesha and her sister Heather, Big Leon, Gavi, and many others. Together, we have changed our world with love and, in the process, learned an important truth:

> *Love isn't love*
> *Till you give it away*
> *You got to give it away.*

It's time to be bold and live the life that Jesus calls us to experience.

Endnotes

Introduction

1. "Emily." Written by Michael W. Smith and Wayne Kirkpatrick. 1987 Milene Music, Inc. (ASCAP), Careers–BMG Music Publishing, Inc. (BMI). All Rights Reserved. Used by Permission.
2. "Live the Life." Written by Micahel W. Smith and Brent Bourgeois. 1997 Milene Music, Inc. (ASCAP), Deer Valley Music (ASCAP), and ADC Music/W.B.M. Corp. (SESAC). All Rights Reserved. Used by Permission.

Chapter 1

1. "Give It Away." Written by Michael W. Smith, Wayne Kirkpatrick, and Amy Grant. 1992 Milene Music, Inc. (ASCAP), Careers–BMG Music Publishing, Inc. (BMI), Magic Beans Music (BMI), and Age to Age Music, Inc. (ASCAP). All Rights Reserved. Used by Permission.
2. "The Other Side of Me." Written by Michael W. Smith and Wayne Kirkpatrick. 1995 Milene Music, Inc. (ASCAP), Deer Valley Music (ASCAP), Careers–BMG Music Publishing, Inc. (BMI) and Magic Beans Music (BMI). All Rights Reserved. Used by Permission.

163

Chapter 2

1. "I'll Lead You Home." Written by Michael W. Smith and Wayne Kirkpatrick. 1995 Milene Music, Inc. (ASCAP), Careers–BMG Music Publishing, Inc. (BMI) and Magic Beans Music (BMI). All Rights Reserved. Used by Permission.

2. "Straight to the Heart." Written by Michael W. Smith and Brent Bourgeois. 1995 Milene Music, Inc. (ASCAP), Deer Valley Music (ASCAP), and ADC Music/ W.B.M. Corp. (SESAC). All Rights Reserved. Used by Permission.

Chapter 3

1. "Breathe in Me." Written by Michael W. Smith and Wayne Kirkpatrick. 1995 Milene Music, Inc. (ASCAP), Deer Valley Music (ASCAP), Careers–BMG Music Publishing, Inc. (BMI) and Magic Beans Music (BMI). All Rights Reserved. Used by Permission.

2. "Picture Perfect." Written by Michael W. Smith and Wayne Kirkpatrick. 1992 Milene Music, Inc. (ASCAP), Careers–BMG Music Publishing, Inc. (BMI), and Magic Beans Music (BMI) All Rights Reserved. Used by Permission.

3. "A Little Stronger Every Day." Written by Michael W. Smith and Wayne Kirkpatrick. 1995 Milene Music, Inc. (ASCAP), Deer Valley Music (ASCAP), Careers–BMG Music Publishing, Inc. (BMI), and Magic Beans Music (BMI). All Rights Reserved. Used by Permission.

Chapter 5

1. "Love One Another." Written by Michael W. Smith and Wayne Kirkpatrick. 1992 Milene Music, Inc. (ASCAP), Careers–BMG Music Publishing, Inc. (BMI), and Magic Beans Music (BMI). All Rights Reserved. Used by Permission.

2. "Calling Heaven." Written by Michael W. Smith and Wayne Kirkpatrick. 1995 Milene Music, Inc. (ASCAP), Deer Valley Music (ASCAP), Careers–BMG Music Publishing, Inc. (BMI), and Magic Beans Music (BMI). All Rights Reserved. Used by Permission.

3. "How Long Will Be Too Long?" Written by Michael W. Smith, Wayne Kirkpatrick, and Amy Grant. 1990 Milene Music, Inc., (ASCAP), Careers–BMG Music Publishing, Inc. (BMI), and Age to Age Music, Inc. (ASCAP). All Rights Reserved. Used by Permission.

Chapter 6

1. "I Will Be Here for You." Written by Michael W. Smith and Diane Warren. 1992 Milene Music, Inc. (ASCAP), and Realsongs (ASCAP). All Rights Reserved. Used by Permission.

Chapter 7

1. "Awesome God." Written by Rich Mullins. Copyright © 1988 Edward Grant, Inc. All Rights Reserved. Used by Permission.

2. "On the Other Side." Written by Michael W. Smith and Wayne Kirkpatrick. 1992 Milene Music, Inc. (ASCAP) and Careers–BMG Music Publishing, Inc. (BMI). All Rights Reserved. Used by Permission.

3. "Cross of Gold." Written by Michael W. Smith and Wayne Kirkpatrick. 1992 Milene Music, Inc. (ASCAP), Careers–BMG Music Publishing, Inc. (BMI), and Magic Beans Music (BMI). All Rights Reserved. Used by Permission.

Chapter 8

1. "The Hand of Providence." Written by Michael W. Smith and Wayne Kirkpatrick. 1988 Milene Music, Inc., (ASCAP),

and Careers–BMG Music Publishing, Inc. (BMI). All Rights Reserved. Used by Permission.

Chapter 9

1. "I Hear Leesha." Written by Michael W. Smith and Wayne Kirkpatrick. 1988 Milene Music, Inc. (ASCAP) and Careers–BMG Music Publishing, Inc. (BMI). All Rights Reserved. Used by Permission.

Chapter 10

1. "Secret Ambition." Written by Michael W. Smith, Wayne Kirkpatrick, and Amy Grant. 1988 Milene Music, Inc. (ASCAP), Careers–BMG Music Publishing, Inc. (BMI) and Riverstone Music, Inc. (ASCAP). All Rights Reserved. Used by Permission.
2. "Somebody Love Me." Written by Michael W. Smith and Wayne Kirkpatrick. 1992 Milene Music, Inc. (ASCAP), Careers–BMG Music Publishing, Inc. (BMI), and Magic Beans Music (BMI). All Rights Reserved. Used by Permission.